WHAT MEN AN
ABOUT *THE MEN'S CODE OF HONOR*...

What a tremendous summation of a "man's man." Dan Stradford brings it all together with penetrating insights and personal notes forming a pathway to guide boys and men in the principles of integrity, fairness and human dignity. I can't wait to share it with the younger men in my family.

Mike Anderson, Juris Doctorate

A must-read for all men. It fills the gap in our prevailing culture, which unfortunately lacks formal rites of passage and codes of behavior for teaching boys to become men. It's what women *really* want! Dan Stradford does a masterful job in this book, well-illustrated with touching stories from his own life (you'll be moved to tears—I was!). For women, too—this is what to look for in a man, one who will care for, cherish, and protect you through thick and thin. Man or woman, you'll be informed, inspired, and I'd say, transformed by this beautifully written book.

Hyla Cass MD, author of *8 Weeks to Vibrant Health* (www.cassmd.com)

The Men's Code of Honor is a much-needed, refreshing, well-written, and concise reminder for today's modern man on how to live and behave honorably in all aspects of life. The book is the manual behind the common cliché, "Act like a man," and perfectly outlines what that phrase means and how to do it. *The Men's Code of Honor* pulls gems from ethical codes all over the world, from a variety of institutions, laws and organizations and unifies them in a simple, applicable code for all men. In today's society, where honor, chivalry, and courage are fading values, *The Men's Code of Honor* should be required reading for all men and also women who need a reminder of how honorable men should act toward them.

>Erin Stair, M.D., West Point Graduate

A book for any man who wants to evolve into the man he always wanted to be. The core values that every man should strive for, support others to attain, and share with those around him are simple, yet sometimes difficult to attain. However, Dan Stradford has given examples from his own life and those of others to make it achievable.

>Kurt Krueger, Teacher and Scout Leader
>President, Healthy Success Systems

Brilliantly written and easy to read. Dan Stradford has done a wonderful job taking the reader on a journey through history and the development of rules of conduct. It is an original and fascinating approach to the way men should conduct themselves, publicly or privately. A must read for all business leaders, public officials, teachers and administrators.

>Joseph Mazin, CEO, Flamemaster Corporation
>and author of *The Dream Master*

"Courage, integrity, loyalty, strength—these are the yardsticks of manhood." This short sentence captures the essence of Dan Stradford's wonderful book, *The Men's Code of Honor*. In a time where our world seems in turmoil and the difference between right and wrong is blurred, comes an honest assessment of what it takes to be an honorable and moral man. Right conduct and moral behavior among men and women is the cornerstone of any highly successful culture. However, this path of right conduct is not always instinctual, and road maps are necessary. Dan's book helps to remind us that our duty as men is to uphold the principles of courage, integrity, loyalty and strength not only for ourselves in the present moment, but for our sons (and daughters) now and in the future. I highly recommend this book.

Kurt Woeller, Doctor of Osteopathy

This book should be required reading for leaders of all ranks. Becoming a man of honor doesn't just happen; it takes a personal commitment to defining what that means, daily personal courage and discipline to choose the harder right over the easier wrong, and the learning that sometimes happens only after stumbling. Dan Stradford's 66 tenets are the answers to the test; I hope this book inspires men everywhere to "raise the bar."

Major Arthur Moore, U.S. Army Infantry,
West Point Class of 2000

This book should be read by any person who has leadership traits or is in a leadership position in the military or any other organization. The tenets are well worth the time to learn and to refer back to as needed.

> Command Sergeant Major (retired) Robert A. Eldredge, Virginia Army National Guard

Dan Stradford has captured the unwritten code of men that we as martial artists and as men constantly work toward. I recommend this book to all men who are striving to live a better life and to be a better man.

> Taylor Jerling, Martial Arts Instructor, Black Belt

The Men's Code of Honor is a powerful and complete list of everything a man knows he should be, looking deep into our minds to find what makes us men, and if need be, how we can correct ourselves to be that man inside.

> Daniel Sinohui, High School Student

Simplicity and elegance, a great guide that is well explained. Every man should have a code. If you are still defining yours, this will be a great source of inspiration. An essential reference to gentlemen of all ages.

> Steve Mitchell, GentlemansCode.com and TheMitchelli.com

THE MEN'S CODE OF HONOR

66 Principles that Make a Man

DAN STRADFORD

Whisper
CANYON

The Men's Code of Honor,
66 Principles that Make a Man
© 2012 by Dan Stradford

Whisper Canyon Publishing
www.whispercanyon.net
info@whispercanyon.net

    Stradford, Dan.
        The men's code of honor / by Dan Stradford.
        p. cm.
        LCCN 2012930522
        ISBN 978-0-9848180-0-6

      1. Men--Conduct of life. 2. Honor.   I. Title.

BJ1601.S77 2012   170.81'1
                              QBI12-600009

All rights reserved. No part of this book may be used or reproduced in whole or in part without written permission from the copyright holder, except in the case of brief passages embodied in critical articles or reviews; nor may any part of this book be reproduced, stored in a retrieval system, or transmitted in any form or by any means electronic, mechanical, photocopying, recording, or other, without written permission from the copyright holder.

To my wonderful wife Betty
for helping me find
the man inside the boy
she married so long ago.

TABLE OF CONTENTS

Introduction		xi
The Men's Code of Honor		xxi
1	Integrity	1
2	Cooperation	25
3	Behavior	39
4	Courage	55
5	Women, Children, and Family	69
6	Work	103
7	Duty	115
8	The False Code	135
9	Becoming a Man of Honor	149
10	Appendix: Codes Referenced	159
	Native American Men's Code of Conduct	159
	West Point Cadet Honor Code	161
	California Institute of Technology Honor Code	161
	U.S. Army Rangers Creed	161
	Boy Scouts of America's Scout Law	162

Military Code of Conduct	165
The Sailor's Creed	166
Core Values of the United States Navy	167
Code of the West (Owen)	168
U.S. Navy Seal Code	169
Code of the West (Bender)	170
The Ten Commandments of the Code of Chivalry	170
The Polish Knights' Movement Regulations	171
Oath of Knighthood	171
The Code of Chivalry	171
L'Ordene de Chavalerie	172
The Extension Workers' Code of 1922	173
Native American Indian Traditional Code of Ethics	173
Native American Code of Ethics (1994)	177
The Articles of John Philips	179
(British) Armed Forces Code of Social Conduct	181
The Rotary Code of Ethics	185
Thirteenth Century Code of Chivalry	185
Gentleman's Code of Conduct	186
Jesuit Athlete's Code of Conduct	188
Benjamin Franklin's Thirteen Virtues of Life	190
Knight's Code of Chivalry	191
The Pirate Code of Conduct	192
Additional Resources	193

INTRODUCTION

"The greatest way to live with honor in this world is to be what we pretend to be." Socrates

SOME YEARS AGO, I was traveling through Utah with some friends and their two boys after having hiked the magnificent, but exhausting, Subway Canyon in Zion National Park. The younger boy asked me something about the way men treat women. I told him that an unspoken code exists among men that we all tend to subscribe to and this guides how we treat women. His father nodded in agreement.

This brief incident passed but the moment stayed with me. Why is it, I wondered, that this "code" is unspoken? Why hasn't anyone written it down?

We regularly hear someone comment about what a "real man" would do, or we hear people ask, "What kind of a man would do that?" And virtually every male has been told at some point in his life to "act like a man." Obviously, we all have an idea of how a "real man" should behave. There are clearly boundaries men are not expected to cross, even if such honorable behavior appears to be vanishing from our society.

Men actually take matters of honor very seriously. These issues determine our standing amongst our family and other men. More so, they are the matters that pass through our minds when we are alone with our thoughts at night and when we face ourselves in the mirror each morning. No boy or man escapes them. Courage, integrity, loyalty, strength—these are the yardsticks of manhood, and every male knows where he stands against that measurement at any given time.

I decided to take on the task of dissecting this Code of Honor that men carry inside themselves, this collection of commandments that we gather over our lifetimes, these somber moments of reflection where we silently commit ourselves to specific rules of manly behavior.

I searched for male codes of conduct down through the ages. Codes of chivalry. Military codes. Academic codes. The Code of the West. The Cowboy's Code. There are lots of them, most restricted to certain professions or groups, but all of them profoundly similar in many of their tenets.

I have drawn from many of these sources, including the following 28 distinct codes, which are each explained and listed in the appendix:

Native American Men's Code of Conduct
West Point Cadet Honor Code
California Institute of Technology Honor Code

Introduction

U.S. Army Rangers Creed

Boy Scouts of America's Scout Law

Military Code of Conduct

The Sailor's Creed

Core Values of the United States Navy

Code of the West (Owen)

U.S. Navy Seal Code

Code of the West (Bender)

The Ten Commandments of the Code of Chivalry

The Polish Knights' Movement Regulations

Oath of Knighthood

The Code of Chivalry

L'Ordene de Chavalerie

The Extension Workers' Code of 1922

Native American Indian Traditional Code of Ethics

Native American Code of Ethics (1994)

The Articles of John Philips

(British) Armed Forces Code of Social Conduct

The Rotary Code of Ethics

Thirteenth Century Code of Chivalry

Gentleman's Code of Conduct

Jesuit Athlete's Code of Conduct

Benjamin Franklin's Thirteen Virtues of Life

Knight's Code of Chivalry

The Pirate Code of Conduct

The Men's Code of Honor

It is evident that certain fundamentals regarding honorable behavior have been chiseled in stone and remained constant down through the ages. Clearly men have a sense inside them of what it means to "act like a man."

Even in our high-tech world of fast and loose relationships where many men think they can avoid the "old" rules of how to act like a man, reality comes crashing down when they make a girl pregnant, face the law for their crimes, or get caught in a lie. Honor still matters.

In addition to reviewing these traditional codes, I asked the following questions to find what drives men on a gut level:

- What are men genetically designed to do?
- What have men traditionally done for thousands of years?
- What do men expect of other men?
- What failings cause a man to feel less of a man?
- What slurs are the most insulting to a man?
- What failings does a man hope that other men won't find out about him?
- What qualities and duties most fit the male physique, physiology, and temperament?
- What rules of conduct are necessary so that typical negative male behavior can be controlled or channeled?
- What do men most commonly try to teach boys?

Introduction

- What does our language emphasize regarding men and boys?

In today's world, much is said about men and women being equal. In the West, few question a woman's intellectual equality or that women can do most of the jobs that men have traditionally done. Perhaps to make up for past injustices, our desire to see women treated as equals has become so zealous that in some circles we are hesitant to state the obvious: Men and women are different.

They don't just have different genitals. They have different body chemistry. They have different brains. They are built for different tasks. (Guys, good luck trying to nurse a baby.) They are genetically programmed to want different things. As an obvious example, most women want to attract men and most men want to attract women.

These structural and genetic differences have programmed men to behave a certain way and react negatively to men who do not behave this way. Most of this programming has to do with survival and perpetuating our offspring and our species. Layered on top of this are our cultural norms. This is where reason has intervened and regulated our baser impulses. Honed over time through trial, error, and much suffering, rules of conduct—honorable conduct—have been forged.

Honor is defined as "integrity in one's beliefs and actions." "Integrity" means a wholeness. One's beliefs match one's actions. Because of cultural differences, not all men subscribe to the exact same concepts of honorable behavior. But their disagreements are remarkably few in general.

Kids raised around criminal elements or adults with bad habits may, at first, idolize gang members or other bad guys. Even kids from good neighborhoods get exposed to rough characters on TV, the Internet, and in movies—or maybe a tough kid down the block—and get the idea it would be cool to be a bad dude.

But from an early age, almost all boys are also exposed to the good guys. They see men who go to work and take care of their families. Not perfect men, perhaps, but men who have clear basic principles to choose right over wrong.

And amongst these men, a boy occasionally finds a truly honorable man, a man who has peered into his own soul many times and made hard decisions to live an honest life. He is visibly a man who not only talks the talk, but walks the walk. He is respected and trusted.

These men of honor sit in tall thrones in the hearts of boys and young men everywhere. Regardless of the boy's upbringing or environment, regardless of whether he's a good kid or a bad one, he knows who this man is and what he represents. He knows that if he has the courage, someday he may be able to walk the road that man has traveled, and if so, it will be a life well lived.

A code of honor is not the same as a moral code or a religious code of behavior. Morals—many laid down by the

Introduction

wisdom of our great religions—dictate what is right and wrong conduct. A moral code spans all the activities of life. A code of honor certainly addresses conduct, and may carry some of the same rules as a moral code, but it is more focused on duty—what are one's inescapable responsibilities in life? "Duty," said General George Patton, "is the essence of manhood."

In the code that follows, we talk freely of "men," "boys," and "males" as if they were all one entity. Nothing could be further from the truth. Men and boys differ dramatically in their views, feelings, intellectual abilities and behaviors. Some are poets, dancers, and actors. Others are rugby players, plumbers, and professional soldiers. Some are hopeless romantics and others are sports addicts. Some have feminine qualities while others are growling, stubble-bearded, whisky-swilling he-men. Men can be short, tall, fat, skinny, religious, hedonistic, furry, and hairless.

So it can be dangerous indeed to speak of men in sweeping generalities. But we have taken this liberty because—in general amongst men—these concepts hold true. Exceptions will exist.

The same is true of women. We will be speaking of men's role as protectors of women and providers for women. Of course, in today's world, women are perfectly capable of providing for and protecting themselves in many instances, so such sweeping generalities may seem to demean women. But it shouldn't. This isn't a book about women. It's about men and their motives and drives. The fact that a woman may not need protecting isn't going to change the fact that men are hardwired to do so.

When people think of honorable men, they may get an image of a handsome gentleman offering his raincoat to a lady in a storm or a soldier braving a hail of bullets to save a comrade. Perhaps. But most men of honor are quite ordinary. They are guys who marry a girl because they got her pregnant, giving up a college diploma to work a factory job to provide for their child. It's the man who works all day and studies all evening to get ahead so he can make a future for his family. It's the boy with a sick mother and no father, who makes sure his younger siblings are dressed, fed, and taken to school.

Not every man seeking to be honorable will necessarily follow every tenet of this code. We are, after all, human. Some fellows are strong in some areas and weak in others. But a great many boys and men struggle against the strains and stresses of life, trying to do the right thing.

There are 66 tenets in the Men's Code of Honor, divided into seven categories. I have followed this with a chapter on what I call a "false code"—those mistaken beliefs perpetuated through time which may sound good at first, but actually make it more difficult to become truly honorable.

With honorable men, it is only natural that, depending on the circumstances and the man, one tenet may take

Introduction

priority over another when they seem to conflict. One man may choose to break his promise, for example, and miss a business appointment to take advantage of having lunch with his daughter to show her his love and support. A different fellow may choose the business appointment to ensure he is earning enough money to provide for his family.

Many honorable men became so by behaving dishonorably. All of us have used poor judgment or behaved irresponsibly and have witnessed the unfortunate consequences of our actions. And we learned. We learned to ask more of ourselves. Thus, honorable behavior is a road of improvement where perfection is never quite within our grasp.

Benjamin Franklin once wrote a moral code for himself but found it impossible to implement all the tenets at once. He settled on working on a single tenet at a time each day—honesty, for example. At first, our men's code may stir up a lot of guilt because it can remind us of how far we have strayed from our ideal principles. Don't let it overwhelm you. Work on it a step at a time.

This Code of Honor is not the final word in men's behavior. It is an attempt to codify what drives us to do right by our girlfriends, wives, children, other men, and fellow humans.

It's a road map that is never quite complete as we work consistently to do our best, so that when death is at our door, we can silently review our travels and, hopefully, say to ourselves, "You did well."

Raising the Bar

In the code that follows, we frequently use such words as "never" and "always." These are strenuous demands, to say that one will never or always follow a certain path and uphold a certain standard. Some men may protest that this is too much to ask.

No, it isn't.

Studies have shown that those who have high expectations of themselves may fail sometimes and their self-demands may be stressful, but they actually achieve more than those who set the bar low.

Those guys who complain, "But man, never be disloyal to my wife? Are you kidding?" No, we're not. Most men are loyal to their wives. Get with the program. Raise the bar, Jack.

Self-discipline is an essential ingredient of honor. It's something men work on throughout their lives. Setting high standards is the first step to letting yourself know that you are serious.

Raise the bar.

Dan Stradford

Introduction

THE MEN'S CODE OF HONOR

INTEGRITY

1. Tell the truth.
2. Keep your word.
3. Mean what you say and say what you mean.
4. Don't make excuses.
5. Admit your mistakes.
6. Take responsibility for your actions.
7. Fulfill your obligations and duties.
8. Finish what you start.
9. Respect and believe in yourself.
10. Don't compromise with your principles.

COOPERATION

11. Respect the law.
12. Play by the rules.
13. Don't take unfair advantage.
14. Don't whine.
15. Respect the property of others.
16. Carry your share of the load.
17. Be fair and just.

BEHAVIOR

18. Don't gossip.
19. Don't bully.

20. Don't be a braggart.
21. Don't pry into other people's business unnecessarily.
22. Harm no one without good cause.
23. Use a firm handshake.
24. Look a person in the eye when you greet him.
25. Do not let anger rule your conduct.
26. Do not let your appetites rule you.

COURAGE

27. Stand tall in the face of adversity.
28. Do what needs to be done.
29. Defend yourself and your interests.
30. Use force as a last resort, then use it well.
31. Be prepared to risk your life or safety for a greater good.
32. Face death with courage.
33. Always stand guard.

WOMEN, CHILDREN, AND FAMILY

34. Honor women and their feminine nature.
35. Never use force against a woman, except in self-defense.
36. Never force sex on anyone.
37. Protect women and children.
38. Do not use crude language in the presence of children.
39. Do not use crude language in the presence of women without their approval.
40. Always be faithful to your romantic partner.
41. Never steal another man's romantic partner.

Introduction

42. Meet the romantic needs of your partner.
43. Love and support children.
44. Provide for your family.
45. Serve your young children's needs before your own.
46. Marry the mother of your children.
47. Make your home a sanctuary of security for your family.
48. Do not unnecessarily burden your family.
49. Don't make your mother cry.
50. Plan and prepare for your family's future.
51. Support actions that make a better world for our children.

WORK

52. Take pride in your work.
53. Don't be lazy.
54. Treat your superiors and elders with respect.
55. Do the hard work, the dirty work, the mechanical work, the dangerous work, and the heavy lifting.
56. Always give an honest day's labor.

DUTY

57. Defend your nation.
58. If called upon to lead, lead with clarity and set standards of discipline and keep them.
59. Be loyal to your family, group, nation and friends.
60. Do not desert a friend or ally.
61. Show compassion and mercy for the weak, the dependent, and the helpless.

The Men's Code of Honor

62. Champion what is right and good.
63. Confront and fight evil.
64. Respect the earth and her life forms.
65. Set a good example.
66. Uphold the tradition of men's honor by expecting other men to be honorable.

1

INTEGRITY

I GREW UP in deep poverty in the city of St. Louis. In the first grade, my mother typically sent me to school with a cold fried egg sandwich, or something even less appetizing, in a crumpled, grease-stained lunch bag that we reused. I'd sit with the other kids at noon on a bench against the wall in the gymnasium, watching them eat their lunchmeat sandwiches, potato chips, Twinkies, and fruit while I hoped they did not notice my meager meal.

One day I decided to steal another kid's lunch. I was delighted to find chips, a snack cake, and a well-made sandwich lovingly cut in half diagonally. I tried to enjoy my meal as I looked about nervously to see if anyone had a clue of my crime.

Not long after, I did it again. But this time I looked up from my stolen food to see the teacher walking along the benches with the robbery victim, scanning each child's lunch to see if the boy could spot the meal his mother had packed. For me, a lifetime passed as they walked slowly by me, looking at my food without comment.

At the age of six, I knew it was wrong to take another kid's lunch, even if I was poor and hungry. As I looked around the gymnasium after the teacher had passed, the room was no longer filled with my playmates. They were now children whose values I had betrayed, who might find out what I had done. I felt like a lost soul.

I never stole a lunch again.

1. **Tell the truth.**

   "Accordingly, we will: Conduct ourselves in the highest ethical manner in all relationships with peers, superiors and subordinates; Be honest and truthful in our dealings with each other, and with those outside the Navy."

   Core Values of the United States Navy

In reviewing men's codes of conduct throughout history, the one rule most of them have in common is to tell the truth.

Telling the truth can require more courage than taking a beating or even taking a bullet. In fact, many a man has committed suicide because he was not brave enough to face people with the truth.

Honesty is the building block of human relations. Without it, all else crumbles.

Bosses depend upon employees to tell them facts so they know what is going on in a business.

Wives need correct information from their husbands on all kinds of matters: How much did you make this week? When are you coming home? Where are you? Are you picking up the kids?

Girlfriends need certainty in a relationship and that starts with a man telling the truth to those many questions: Will you call me tomorrow? Where were you last night? Are you dating anyone else?

Men who lie or tell half-truths are looked down upon by other men. And they are disliked by most women. One lie can ruin a relationship for years or even forever.

Men who tell the truth are prized, especially if they always tell the truth. That's the person you can truly have confidence in. That's the person who will give you a straight answer, even if it makes him look bad.

A liar puts others at risk. He gives them false information to operate on. He wastes their time as they end up having to track down the true data. He betrays their trust in him.

Lying is, in fact, an act of cowardice. People do it because they are afraid to face the consequences of telling the truth.

Sometimes telling the truth hurts you because you have to admit a wrongdoing or a mistake. You could have to take the blame and it could cost you money or time to fix the mess you made if you say what really happened—for example, in a car accident. An honest man has the courage to tell the truth anyway. He knows that by being honest he makes the world a better place. He knows that lying will create bitterness and upset in other people who would no longer trust him. He also knows that honest behavior sets an example to the people he is involved with so, hopefully, they, too, will be inspired to tell the truth.

Many people say they want peace in their lives or a peaceful world. Peace starts with telling the truth. There is no peace amongst liars because they don't trust each other.

With honest people problems tend to resolve easily, because no one is denying responsibility. There is no arguing over who is at fault because no one is trying to avoid blame.

If you are a man who lies occasionally or often, the personal decision to start telling the truth can be one of the most transformational events in your life.

Of course, sometimes telling the truth can hurt someone's feelings, such as a wife asking her husband, "Do I look fat?" Or a child showing her father some scribbles, calling it a flower, and asking for his praise. Common sense tells us to use tact and there is no reason to hurt someone's feelings just so you can be truthful.

But make sure you're not fooling yourself. Cowards often use this as an excuse to lie: "I didn't tell my girlfriend I was dating someone else because I didn't want to hurt her feelings." Guys like this are lying because they lack the courage to face up to their own dishonest acts.

Integrity

Also, a man can sometimes find himself in an adversarial situation, such as in the military, where he does not want to give information to an enemy. Telling the truth may not be the greatest good in that situation. But again, be careful of this excuse because lots of men see their boss, wife, or even friends as "the enemy" to whom they can't tell the truth.

Sometimes you may not want to tell someone the truth. Instead of lying, an honest man simply says what he feels. He might state, "I'd rather not say. It's a personal matter." Or something else that is an honest answer but still maintains his privacy.

Commonly we also lie to ourselves. Coming clean with yourself requires courage, but men through the ages have often changed their lives dramatically for the better by doing just that.

Be an honest man. Tell the truth.

2. Keep your word.

"A Scout is Trustworthy. A Scout tells the truth. He is honest, and he keeps his promises. People can depend on him."

Boy Scouts of America's Scout Law

A story is told of a wealthy man who sold one of his companies for $50,000,000. However, the buyer of the company took longer than expected—six months—to get all the legal work done to make the purchase. By then the company had grown dramatically. It was now worth $250,000,000. The embarrassed buyer, feeling responsible for the delay, asked the seller if he now wanted more money for the company.

The wealthy man said no. He had sold it for $50,000,000 and—regardless of the delay—he felt he had given his word on the price and that was the end of it.

A man who keeps his word is more valuable than gold.

Few things create more upset than broken promises. A father who misses his son's big basketball game when he said he'd come. A fellow worker who doesn't get the truck loaded in time as he swore he would. An adult son who cancels a fishing date his aging dad was looking forward to.

A man could be smart, capable, and have a great personality. But if he doesn't show up when he's supposed to, he's pretty useless. If he doesn't do what he said he would do, he is of limited value. People will always wonder if he'll disappoint them again. So they decide not to depend on him anymore.

The girlfriend decides to drop this fellow because he's not reliable—not the qualities she wants to see in a potential husband or father. His friends don't invite him to social events because they are sick of waiting for a guy who never shows up. His relatives never ask him to do anything important because they know how undependable he is.

As a result, the man who doesn't keep his word gets little respect from his friends and family. He doesn't advance in his job or career because he's considered too careless. And he loses girlfriends or goes through divorce because he's broken too many promises.

But let's look at the guy who keeps his word, no matter what. Everyone respects him because they know they can depend on him. They know that if this guy said he will do it, it is as good as done.

That's the guy bosses go to for important projects. That's the kind of man a woman knows will make a dependable husband. That's what a kid wants to see in his dad. And that's what we all want in a friend.

Keeping your word can be hard sometimes. It may mean all types of sacrifices, like working longer hours or driving someplace late at night or having to give up your day off. A man should still make every effort to deliver on his promises.

Eyes are upon you. Show them you deliver the goods. Keep your word.

3. Mean what you say and say what you mean

"A knight must have truth in one's heart and mouth."

The Polish Knights' Movement Regulations

Confidence is a vital part of being a man—not only confidence in himself but ensuring that others have confidence in him.

One of the most important things a man can do to generate that bond of trust is to mean what he says and say what he means.

Let's look at the two parts of this concept.

Mean what you say.

Men who say things they don't really mean are considered insincere. If they pay you a compliment, it feels slimy. When such a father tells his son they'll go to a baseball game, the kid knows it probably won't happen and he's disgusted. If a policeman has a guy like this for a partner, he worries when this man tells him, "I've got your back."

Don't say something unless you mean it. Don't flatter people with false compliments like, "Have you lost weight?" or "I love that dress." If it isn't true, don't say it. Why? Because when you tell your wife or girlfriend, "You look beautiful," you want her to know you mean it. The only way she will know it is if she is sure you are a man who doesn't say something unless he feels it's true. The only way she'll know this is if you always mean what you say.

Don't tell your kid, "I'll be back," if you won't. Don't tell a girl or woman, "I'll call you tomorrow," if you won't. Show the courage it takes to explain to that kid or woman that you won't be back or won't call.

"But they'll get mad at me," you say. Of course, they might. And you'll have to deal with that and talk the matter out with them. That takes guts. Show some. Be forthright with the people you deal with. To do otherwise shows a lack of respect for them and yourself.

Your word is your bond. It carries a lot of power, but only if others know you mean it. You want them to know with absolute certainty that that's what you think and intend. They can take it to the bank. It's the real deal because you said it.

Say what you mean.

Guys who are not straightforward, who are mealy-mouthed and afraid to get to the point, look weak and, frankly, irritating to others. People tend to doubt them and question what they are saying.

There's no need to be evasive or unclear. Even a five-year-old boy can give it to you straight.

Sure, it can be hard to be open and honest when you're under stress or you feel awkward about a situation or about telling the truth. And some situations require tact so you minimize hurt feelings. Do the best you can. But don't tell partial truths, leave out important details, or minimize the facts so you can weasel out of an uncomfortable circumstance.

Be the kind of man you want for a friend, someone who tells you the facts and what he thinks. He can do it with kindness and support, trying to avoid hurt feelings, but he tells it like it is.

People don't want to deal with a man who doesn't stand behind what he says. Mean what you say and say what you mean.

4. Don't make excuses.

"Exhibit courage in word and deed."

Code of Chivalry

Few things look as unmanly as a fellow who makes excuses for his actions, failures and behavior.

In a military unit, no one wants to hear, "I fell asleep on duty but it wasn't my fault because...."

On a professional baseball team, the other men don't want to listen to, "I dropped the ball because the fans were booing me."

Of course, some things in life are out of our control or unexpected and because of this, at times, we cannot reach our goals despite our best efforts. But there is a big difference between a man who runs into insurmountable obstacles and a guy who simple didn't do his job.

Integrity

One of the quickest ways that men measure other men is by how they handle responsibility. If a guy makes a mistake and responds with, "Sorry, my fault. I won't let it happen again," the other men will likely give him another chance. This guy stepped up and knows he's causing his own errors.

But if they hear, "I tried but I have this headache and I've been so busy lately, blah, blah, blah...," they know they have an excuse-maker on their hands. This guy won't take responsibility for much of anything. And he'll finger-point and blame when the going gets rough. In a group of real men, this guy is baggage.

How refreshing it is to a wife, customer, or military commander to have a man step forward and say, "I was responsible for causing this," or "I was supposed to make this happen and I failed to do so."

A man who makes excuses is telling the world that he is not responsible for his actions. He is saying that if he promises something or has commitments or duties, that it's OK for him to fail at these and abandon his obligations because it's never his fault. Someone else is always to blame. Or the weather. Or whatever.

You can't depend on this man. No one can. He will likely fail and disappoint often because he doesn't have enough control over his own actions to even acknowledge that he is causing them.

Don't be that guy. Don't lie to yourself and say it wasn't your responsibility when it was. If you failed those who depend on you, have the courage to own up to that. It might be embarrassing for the moment, but those around you will know that you take your obligations seriously and will likely give you another chance to make it right.

5. Admit your mistakes.

A knight shall have "the ability to admit fault, when proved wrong."

Thirteenth Century Code of Chivalry

This is the other side of "Don't make excuses."

One of the most difficult things a man can do is face others after he has failed them, wasted their time or money, caused damage or harm, or made some other horrific error. This requires courage. It requires facing the disappointment and wrath of those you have wronged.

Own up to your mistakes or failures. "I tried but just couldn't make it happen."

"I failed to see the enemy cross over the border, sir."

"I know you entrusted me with getting the sales up but I failed to do that."

"I promised you I wouldn't use drugs again but I have."

Some men think it's a sign of weakness to admit they are wrong. They also fear it will make them look bad or incompetent and reduce their stature in the eyes of their kids, wife, employer or others. Maybe it will, but this is who you are. This is reality. Not acknowledging your mistakes is a form of lying. And in the long run, the price of a dishonest life is far worse.

People highly regard a man who can admit his mistakes. It shows he has courage. It shows he has enough self-confidence that he can take the punch of exposing his own shortcomings. And it shows he respects the people around him and is being a team member by taking responsibility and not falsifying his statements regarding what happened.

Most important, a man who admits his errors can then fix them. The first step to improving oneself is accepting that one is flawed in the first place.

Of course, in a legal matter you may be instructed by your attorney to not admit fault. How you choose to deal with that is your call. But that's a rare instance. In everyday living, you have a responsibility to be honest when you mess up.

Pity the guy who won't admit his mistakes. He spends his days and nights in his own hell, explaining repeatedly to himself and others why it's not his fault that he fails at this and that. And he can never climb out of the hole because he doesn't have the backbone to tell himself or others what he actually knows—that he's responsible for what goes on in his life.

6. Take responsibility for your actions.

"We will...abide by an uncompromising code of integrity, taking responsibility for our actions and keeping our word."

The Core Values of the United States Navy

This is the next step up from "Admit your mistakes."

It's a good thing to admit you did something wrong, but now you have to fix it. Thomas Jefferson once said, "It is more honorable to repair a wrong than to persist in it."

Every once in a while we hear a politician or famous name come clean publicly about some scandal he's involved in. You'll hear him say, "I take full responsibility." But then he does nothing about it. Saying you are taking responsibility is not the same as making up for what you did wrong.

You walk in the door and your wife says, "Did you pick up the bread at the store like I asked?" Your shoulders sag. You're beat. You were looking forward to plopping down on the couch for a while. But the answer is, no, you forgot to pick up the bread. What do you do?

A guy with no self respect yells at his wife for making him go to the store when she knows how busy he is, blah, blah, blah.

An honorable man knows he told his wife he'd pick up the bread and that he must honor his commitments. He needs to take responsibility for his failure to stop at the store. Maybe he'll get lucky and his wife will say it's not important so he can let it go. Either way, he has to be ready to fulfill his promise without complaint.

Taking responsibility for one's actions, however, can require a lot more nerve than driving to the store. You get a girl pregnant. You damage someone's car. You make a mistake that costs your employer a lot of money. These are the things that separate cowards from honorable men.

The coward abandons his responsibilities. He runs out of town or tries to cover up his connection to the disaster. The man of honor not only admits his responsibility for the incident but offers to make amends if at all possible. He doesn't just leave people hanging with the wreckage of his mistakes.

Sure, this can cost you terribly, in terms of time, money, and other sacrifices, to remedy your wrongs. But the other choice is that you leave others with these same burdens—to repair a wrecked car, to raise a fatherless child—caused by something you did.

The world is strewn with the damage careless men have caused and left behind. It costs individuals and society a fortune and untold heartbreak to clean up messes caused by irresponsible guys who abandon those they have wronged.

Even if a man makes a mistake, he earns a lot of respect when he says, "I did it. What do I need to do to fix it?"

7. Fulfill your obligations and duties.

"We will...fulfill or exceed our legal and ethical responsibilities in our public and personal lives twenty-four hours a day."

The Core Values of the United States Navy

Life is filled with obligations and duties. Boys often have duties like mowing the lawn or taking out the trash or watching over their younger brothers or sisters. Men have obligations to their families, their jobs, legal authorities, and many others.

Sometimes the load gets pretty heavy. But if you have agreed to a duty or it has been assigned to you by life (such as an eldest son having to care for his siblings), treat it as a sacred trust. Take the vow that it WILL get done.

When someone doesn't carry out his duties, the system breaks down and trouble happens. Few things feel as disappointing as when everyone is depending on a fellow to do his job and he doesn't. It is a man's duty to see that this doesn't occur. Take the viewpoint that you will not fail those who depend on you.

Let us say you are supposed to take your son to soccer practice but you're tired. Or you have signed up to serve in the military only to find out shortly after that a war has started. Or you promised your dying father you'd care for your mother and she calls you for help at 3 AM. Or you agreed to work the first weekend of every month and later realize that includes Super Bowl Sunday. Or you took a vow to stand by your wife through sickness and health and she later becomes a paraplegic.

Every day men have to make decisions about these matters.

Do your job, even if it doesn't seem fair. Be a rock to those you have obligations to. Let them know by your steady dependability that they can count on you, no matter what.

This applies to your employment. Most people have many duties to their employers. Do them. Carry them out. Don't let your fellow workers or employer down.

This applies to your family. If you have an obligation to help your parents, your wife, your kids, or anyone else, make sure you carry that through.

This applies to your role as a citizen. You have taxes to pay. Laws to obey. Perhaps military duty to serve.

Where families, businesses, and countries are successful, part of the reason is because men step up and fulfill their obligations.

This is what honorable men do.

8. Finish what you start.

"Always finish what you start."

Code of the West (James Owen)

This applies to important matters. We start a lot of things like crossword puzzles, books or hobbies. No one gets hurt if you don't finish them.

But the important things count. And only you will know what those things are. Some projects or actions in your life are significant to you, and you just don't feel right unless you complete them. You could also have obligations to others that can only be fulfilled by finishing something you started.

As an example, for some people, finishing college might not be necessary because they realize they are not academics, they go on to other careers, or whatever. For others, however, completing a university education may be very important and something they will regret if they don't get it done.

Perhaps you want to get your contractor's license. Or you want to fund your kid's college tuition. Maybe you start to build a new home for your family. Or you have a strong need to see if you can play music professionally. It could be that you want to start your own business.

If you start it, finish it. Do what you have to do to tough it out, clear out the barriers, and take it to a "done." Don't let yourself down.

You don't want your life to be haunted by the things you started but never completed. You don't want to be the guy with half-done projects scattered all over his life, who never brings things to fruition.

Make it happen. Not only will this make your life far more satisfying, but it will dramatically build your self-esteem. Finishing what you start will make you the kind of man that you respect and others can rely on.

9. Respect and believe in yourself.

"For it is known that a proud man directed by his honour needs respect for himself and to earn this respect he follows the principles of the holy knightly rule in his life."

Polish Knights' Movement Regulations

Self-confidence may be the most important quality men and boys want to see in themselves. Males who lack self-assurance are, quite frankly, tortured souls. This strikes at the heart of manhood. You feel you are not the man or boy you could and should be, and you are embarrassed by what other men would think about this if they knew.

Men who are uncertain of themselves attract women less. They are poor leaders because they do not inspire confidence in their followers. They accomplish less because they do not have the belief in themselves required to push through the dark forces of life that pressure a man to doubt himself.

It is your duty to yourself to believe in who you are and what you can do and be. Self-doubt is not just an enemy to you. It is destructive to all who believe in and depend on you.

But self-confidence does not come easily to all men. Most men build it gradually as they become more capable and successful from boyhood to manhood. Some men are plagued by feelings of inadequacy no matter how much competence they demonstrate. And still others have grandiose notions of themselves when they are, in fact, quite mediocre.

If you are young, some self-doubt is normal. Self-confidence is usually built on a steady increase in achievement. A man or boy sees his athletic prowess, earning capability, or skills improve over time. He becomes more confident in what he can do and achieve and a calm certainty becomes part of his bearing after a while.

It is important to be able to look at yourself and question your character or lack of skill and knowledge to see if it can be improved. But it is equally important that you know with certainty what is right and good about yourself and that you acknowledge these qualities.

Self-respect is another critical quality that all men want. While some men have exaggerated views of themselves, this usually stems from a lack of self-confidence and respect. True self-respect comes from being the boy or man that you feel you should be and from following your personal values.

10. Don't compromise with your principles.

"Those who stand for nothing, fall for anything."

Alexander Hamilton

A man without principles is not much of a man at all.

Our principles are decisions we have made during our life or concepts that we have come to accept that are used as guidelines for living. They help us deal with the hard choices and impulses of being human. If we have values, we don't have to wonder what to do when faced with sexual temptation, an opportunity to steal or murder, the desire for vengeance, an impulse to be lazy, and many other crossroads of decision. Our principles guide us so we live happier lives that serve the greatest good.

Men can live honorable lives yet differ greatly on some of their principles. Men of honor belong to all political views, nationalities, and religions. They come to their values through their culture, upbringing, education, and personal observations.

Whatever your principles are, if you truly believe in them, you need to live them.

If you are a vegetarian on philosophical grounds, because you don't believe in killing animals, then stand on those principles. Don't eat hamburgers to avoid being embarrassed in front of your friends.

If you are a devout Christian and you hold values that tell you not to drink alcohol, then don't drink just to be sociable.

If you are a member of the military in an ambush and you have a commitment to leave no man behind, then stick to your guns—literally—until your buddies have been brought out of harm's way.

Men who don't practice what they believe to be right usually feel guilty about it. They know in their hearts they are living a lie or that they are not being true to themselves. This lessens their self-respect and sense of honor. It's not a healthy way to go through your days.

It also sends the wrong message to others. They will often conclude that if you don't follow some of your own values, then you likely fall short on others as well, like honesty and reliability.

If you publicly support a principle but secretly don't follow it because you are unsure of it, you need to work it out with yourself what you really believe. Don't let that situation go on. Don't be a man who tells others, for example, of the importance of giving to charity if you don't believe it in your heart. Work out what you truly believe about the matter and then practice what is true for you.

It is normal for a man's values to change as he ages. It's not necessarily wrong for a boy or man to find himself questioning something he has believed much of his life. That's part of personal growth and maturing. But when you reach such a phase, try to sort out what your values should be.

A man or boy needs a clear understanding of what he believes is right and wrong so he can make sound decisions he feels comfortable with when faced with life's challenges.

Once you have it worked out, once you have decided what your values are, do your best to embody them in your life.

2

COOPERATION

When I was eight years old, I met a boy my age named Mike. Mike was every mother's worst nightmare but he fascinated me.

I rarely saw his father but he had uncles who worked in a local carnival. He knew a lot about adult habits and talked to me about drinking, gambling, and sex. Mike showed me how to smoke cigarettes, something he wanted to do almost every day, though I could never master inhaling at that young age. And how do kids get cigarettes? They steal them.

But Mike didn't just slip a cigarette from his mother's purse. He taught me how to steal packs from "confectioneries" in the neighborhood, small stores similar to 7-11s. We'd work together and, while I distracted the person at the counter, Mike reached over it or stepped behind it and grabbed a pack.

Mike also knew another source of cigarettes—parked cars. Most cars were unlocked when I was young. Drivers commonly left their cigarettes on the dashboard or the front seat. Mike showed me that it was a simple matter to open a car door, grab the cigarettes, and smoothly walk away.

One day we snatched a pack from a car, but this time all did not go well. A man yelled at us from across the street. We ran. And we ran. Three blocks later the man had me by the scruff of the neck. Mike surrendered. The police were called.

Despite my faults, my parents had raised me to understand the values of our religion and always thought of me as a "good boy." But now I was taken to a place I would never have imagined I would find myself, a police station. I was questioned over and over. I was afraid they would tell my school principal. I was afraid of what all my relatives would think. And worst of all, my mother had to come and get me.

My crimes had been exposed. For the first time, I saw my deeds through the eyes of others and it was a shameful image. Though no charges were brought against me, I thought that I now had a criminal record. I discovered there was a steep price for breaking the law. I did not see myself the same after that.

My mother's good son was no more.

11. Respect the law.

"Obedience to lawful authority is the foundation of manly character."

Robert E. Lee

Cooperation

Laws are created so that we can live in a safe and functioning environment. Without laws against stealing, murder, tax evasion or other matters, we would have dangerous surroundings where the government doesn't function. Just look at some third world countries where corrupt governments and drug lords rule.

The only way a society can run smoothly is if its citizens respect law and order.

Men have a duty to try to obey the laws of the land. Additionally, boys and other men may be watching your example. If you flaunt the legal system, you are telling them it is OK to do the same. This corrupts your world a little or a lot.

Part of a man's inherent obligation is to make his vicinity safe. Most law enforcement personnel are men. We are protectors of our families and our society. When you disrespect the law by driving at reckless speeds, illegally burning leaves, or beating someone up, you add danger to your surroundings instead of reducing it. And you go against one of the basic duties of manhood, which is to maintain security.

Even if you think a law is silly, it's your job to make all efforts to abide by it. We don't get to pick and choose which laws we want to obey. There is no honor in saying, "I'm not going to obey that law because I don't agree with it." For the society's sake, we must abide by the whole package.

Some laws are never enforced in various cultures. In some cities, for example, it is normal for traffic to run ten miles per hour or more above the speed limit. For whatever reasons, law enforcement officials decide to be lenient with some issues. Common sense will tell you to take that into consideration.

Men who break the law cost all of us hugely. Police spend their days tracking these guys down and investigating them. Our courts are filled with their cases. Our prisons and jails are overflowing with these guys. Families lose their fathers, sons, brothers, and uncles to penitentiaries. Wives and girlfriends lose their partners. Parents and children of these men are heartbroken and sometimes never get over losing a loved one who was incarcerated because he thought he was above the law.

And then there is all the damage they do. They steal from, maim, or murder innocent people. They rape and assault women. They rob from businesses or their government. They drive off with your car or break into your home. They cause your taxes to go up because they don't pay theirs or they require so much government intervention to stop them from their crimes.

And of course, these fellows live in anxiety much of the time, wondering if and when they will get caught.

Don't be part of this. These are men who hurt and betray what is good in the world. It's the very opposite of what is needed from a man.

Show respect for the law. Achieve your goals legally.

12. Play by the rules.

"The athlete must obey all team rules given to him by his coach in a particular sport."

Jesuit Athlete's Code of Conduct

Sometimes there are no laws governing a situation, but there are rules. They could be rules for a card game, a sport, or maybe a group you belong to.

There is no honor in winning by cheating. Play by the regulations. Do what everyone else is obliged to do. This way, if you win, your victory is genuine and something you can be proud of.

Look at athletes who secretly use illegal drugs to pump up their strength. When the truth comes out, they have to hang their heads in shame. Fans lose respect for them. People question whether they honestly earned any of their achievements.

Consider poker players who cheat at cards. When they are discovered, they are kicked out of the game and, if they are amongst a rough crowd, they could face a beating or worse.

And even in a gardening club, where people compete for growing the best roses and such, if a man is found using an illegal hormone to make his plants look better, his fellow competitors feel utterly betrayed when his deception is uncovered. He may never be allowed to compete again.

Rules are agreements. They are promises to those you are participating with that you will perform by the same restrictions and standards as everyone else.

Uphold those standards. Make your participation worthy of respect. Play by the rules.

13. Don't take unfair advantage.

"No member of the Caltech community shall take unfair advantage of any other member of the Caltech community."

California Institute of Technology Honor Code

Sometimes there are no laws OR rules in a matter, but in your heart you know what is the right thing to do.

You're a teenager and you hang out with a younger kid. You know this kid is easy to push around. You go to his house to play a video game, and you get him to make a bet that, if you win, he has to give you the video game. Of course, you end up winning it from him.

You're dating a woman or girl for the first time and you go to a party. She drinks too much. You decide to have sex with her while she's in a confused state.

Your boss doesn't show up at the office and you realize there is no one looking over your shoulder to ensure you do your job. So you decide to goof off.

Cooperation

A man loses his wallet and you find it. It has several hundred dollars in it. You return it to him but tell him that there was no money in it when you found it.

Throughout our lives we are faced with situations where we can take unfair advantage of someone if we want. Don't.

One of the principles of the code of knighthood—which we will address fully later—was to show compassion and mercy for the weak, the dependent, and the helpless. Part of our duties as men is to protect the unprotected and vulnerable. Why? Because we have the strength to do so.

To take unfair advantage of someone means you see they are vulnerable and, instead of showing compassion, you prey on them. It is the opposite of what is needed from you.

This doesn't mean you can't take advantage of many competitive situations that arise in sports, business, military actions, etc., where you see an opportunity and capitalize on it. This happens all the time and is an important element in success and victory.

But to prey on someone in a way that is not fair or just—and you will know when it isn't fair—this is not the way to get ahead in life. You will leave behind a lot of upset people and will become a man not to be trusted. And down the road, you may have a lot of regrets that you will have to reconcile with yourself.

14. Don't whine.

"Never grumble. It makes you about as welcome as a sidewinder in a cow camp."

The Code of the West (Texas Bix Bender)

One of the things men like least in their midst is a guy who is a whiner and complainer.

Life is tough. It's tough for all of us, regardless of your age, income, marital status, religion, or nationality.

We all face bad weather, cars breaking down, accidents, tragedy in our lives, losses, bad luck, betrayal, family problems—you name it. If you have to communicate about rough conditions or a situation, go ahead. We often have to talk about problems in order to solve them. You may be in pain or in fear or have a difficult time dealing with a matter and you want to tell people. Maybe you need to blow a little steam or get things off your chest. There's nothing wrong with that.

But some guys just want to gripe. The pay is too low. The referee was unfair. The traffic is too slow. His wife nags him too much. These guys are usually not interested in solving problems, just complaining about them.

This is unmanly. A man is expected to deal with things or at least try. Whining means you're not even trying and you're making it everyone else's problem. It means you're backing away from your inherent duty to be responsible for your life and you're dumping it all on others.

15. Respect the property of others.

"Touch nothing that belongs to someone else (especially Sacred Objects) without permission, or an understanding between you."

Native American Indian Traditional Code of Ethics

The only way we can live peacefully amongst other people is if we respect each other's property. It is a man's duty—and a duty that goes back to ancient times—to support the respect of property so that we have a world that is safe and secure for all of us.

Don't trespass on someone's land. Don't mess with a car that isn't yours. If you borrow something, bring it back. Don't use someone's equipment without his permission.

16. Carry your share of the load.

"Never shall I fail my comrades. I will always keep myself mentally alert, physically strong, and morally straight and I will shoulder more than my share of the task whatever it may be, one hundred percent and then some."

U.S. Army Rangers Creed

Many a man has gone to bed with a guilty conscience because he did not carry his share of the load. This is one of those things that can quickly make a male feel like he is not the man he should be.

It is not uncommon for a man to go into a deep depression when he's lost his job, causing him to collect unemployment or forcing his wife to support the family on her salary alone.

Pity the guy who fumbles on a critical play in a big game. He didn't do his part and he knows it and it will eat at him.

Whatever the load is, we commonly have to share it. We all have our parts to play. Do yours.

You may see that the sales are down at work and you're one of the salesmen. Make sure you are making your share of the sales and, if not, work diligently on fixing the problem.

As a young man, you may have a single mom who has to work all day and take care of the family when she gets home. Do your share. Help her with the chores, cooking, or whatever, to ensure the labor is not all on her shoulders.

You may have sick or elderly parents who need care. Share the responsibilities with your siblings so no one gets stuck with the full burden.

In the ancient world, if a man didn't carry his share, he didn't survive. In modern times, some men find ways to get away with dumping their duties. They fake injuries to collect disability payments, they go on unemployment and never look for work, they file bogus insurance claims—all kinds of scams so they don't have to earn their own way. These men have lost their self-respect. They are a drain on the hardworking people around them and they know it. They don't have much sense of self-worth and certainly no sense of honor.

If you see a situation where you need to chip in your efforts, do so. Don't leave others to carry your share. You'll feel a lot better about yourself and make life better for those around you.

17. Be fair and just.

"I am committed to excellence and the fair treatment of all."

The Sailor's Creed

An oppressive environment is one in which fairness or justice is absent. Some of history's most respected leaders are considered so because they were fair and just. They asked for reasonable taxes. They used reasonable punishment that fit the crime. They did not assume someone was guilty without proof.

Men often find themselves in positions of leadership, be they fathers, employers, military commanders, coaches or a thousand other supervising positions. The highest compliment such men are often paid is, "He was just and fair."

But leaders are not the only ones who deal in justice. All of us are called upon to pass judgment in our lives. We have to determine guilt or innocence or consequences in a wide array of circumstances.

Men have to make such decisions with their friends, wives, children, family members, girlfriends, co-workers, church members, professional colleagues, teammates, and even strangers. We are called upon to divide up rewards or responsibilities. We have to listen to a person present his case as he defends himself. We have people ask us for help, mercy, understanding or leniency.

You must be fair and just. This brings peace and security to an environment because people feel they can go about their lives without being cheated or mistreated.

In a car accident, tempers often flare and people want to lay blame on others. If it's your accident, make an honest appraisal of the situation and pay for the damages if you are at fault or only ask for what you deserve if the other guy is responsible.

When our children appear to disappoint us, hear them out. Listen to all sides and, if there are penalties to be paid, ensure they are fair.

If someone has broken one of your possessions, weigh all the facts. Maybe this is a good friend to whom you owe a lot so you tell him not to worry about it. Maybe the object was close to breaking when you lent it out so you let the matter go. Or perhaps this was something of value to you so you work out a solution that is fair to both sides.

Cooperation

A longstanding standard of fairness is to treat people the way you want to be treated. Or treat them as if they were your own sons, daughters, or parents.

Of course, dishonest people often complain about any kind of justice, even if it's fair. Treat them fairly anyway. They get the same rewards and penalties as anyone else. This way everyone around you will know you as a fair man.

3

BEHAVIOR

When I was ten years old, my mother had to make a difficult decision. She had four children but not enough money to feed us. She called my Aunt Katherine, who had ten children of her own with another on the way, who graciously agreed to let me live with her for a while.

Contrary to the rough neighborhoods I'd grown up in, my aunt lived in a pleasant, middle-class area where she managed a remarkably organized household on her janitor-husband's salary. Meals were regular and on time as were bedtime and chores. But most inspiring to me was her son Jim.

Jim was fourteen years old and a freshman in high school. He was a great athlete. He introduced me to baseball, took me to my first Cardinals game (and many more), explained sports to me, helped me with my homework, taught me about the marching music of John Philip Sousa, shared his Spanish lessons from school, exposed me to trumpet playing, and much, much more.

I had never known a guy like him. I watched how people loved and respected him, girls and boys, because he was giving, decent, and worked to achieve excellence in all his endeavors. As New Year's Day approached, I made a vow to myself to try to shed the rough edges of my upbringing and be more like this person whom I admired so much.

Jim went on to become a Baptist preacher and now loves his life as a minister to the needy in Colorado for the Salvation Army. He was and remains my hero. Jim never tried to teach me a single lesson about living but, by example, he opened my eyes to the meaning and rewards of an honorable life.

Behavior matters.

18. Don't gossip.

"Speak not but what may benefit others or yourself."

Benjamin Franklin's Thirteen Virtues of Life

Gossip is the practice of passing along juicy bad news about family members, neighbors, friends, co-workers, etc. Joe is going through a divorce. Miguel's daughter is in rehab. Ed is having money problems. Janet may be cheating on her husband.

Gossip has traditionally been considered a habit of women, but men can wag their tongues just as easily.

Behavior

Such tattling looks particularly unseemly on a man. It makes him look weak. He needs to tear others down to make himself feel better. A man's strength should be built on proud accomplishment and self-certainty, not on the tragedies of other people's lives.

Sometimes we have to relay negative information, for example, if a family member has an addiction problem or a friend needs a place to stay because his wife kicked him out of the house. Also, men often participate in competitive circumstances like business, sports, and military situations where bad news for your opponent means good news for you. It's understandable that such data gets passed along.

But a lot of the bad news we hear about people's private suffering has no meaningful value to anyone. It should stop at your ears. There's no need to revel in it and broadcast it to the world.

If a man gossips to you, don't encourage it and don't pass it on. Your job is to provide safety and security to your environment and preying on your friends' and family's weaknesses does not forward that purpose.

19. Don't bully.

> "A Scout knows there is strength in being gentle. He treats others as he wants to be treated. Without good reason, he does not harm or kill any living thing."

Boy Scouts of America's Scout Law

Boys and men know all about domination. We live with it every day in all of its variations. We are hardwired to dislike and fight against it. Males particularly hate to be shamed by public domination. Prison rape is so utterly damaging to the male psyche because it is seen by most men as one of the worst of shames, the near ultimate in domination of one man over another.

As much as men hate domination by others, they are genetically programmed to dominate. These primitive drives push us to win at sports and business. They power us to get through school, get higher paying jobs, win the prettiest girl, be the best provider for our families, ward off intruders, and put our foot down when children go astray.

As we all know, however, primitive drives are not rational ones, so men spend most of their lives learning—and often re-learning—to balance their urges with reason and compassion. One of the early battles we face in our lives is dealing with the urge to bully. Bullying is domination over someone simply because he or she is weaker or different.

A male's most prominent feature is his strength. We are usually stronger than females and most other animals. Men are stronger than boys and older boys are stronger than younger boys. Put a group of young boys together and within minutes you will commonly see some demonstration of strength, some move to show domination. On an animalistic level, the simplest way for a man or boy to demonstrate his strength to himself or others—to show

Behavior

his ability to dominate—is to rough up people weaker than him.

Not all boys and men are chronic bullies, but almost all have pushed around weaker people at some point in their lives. Some prey on girls and women with physical or verbal abuse.

These same primitive awakenings to be strong, to rule—these same forces dictate that we not bully. Rational people understand that a man does not prove his strength by picking on those weaker than him. In fact, it makes him look weak because he can't prove his manliness through ordinary achievement such as excelling at sports, hard work, music, and other such things.

Studies have shown that people who are bullied often carry the scars of it into later life. Don't be part of this. You are a protector. Your purpose is to provide a secure environment where decent people don't have to live in fear. Help that along by resisting the urge to push people around.

20. Don't be a braggart.

"Have virtue even though tempted to brag about the love of your own achievements."

Thirteen Century Code of Chivalry.

A braggart is someone who routinely talks about all his successes. His money, his beautiful girlfriend, his car, his athletic ability, his toughness—you name it and guys like to brag about it.

A little tooting of your own horn is not a bad thing because it's understandable to want to share your accomplishments with others or let potential employers, mates, girlfriends, teammates, etc., know what you are capable of.

But the braggart doesn't want to stop. This guy wants to make other men feel small by comparison to him. He wants others to think he's far more important or capable than them. In actual truth, he's insecure about himself so he needs to blare out his successes—often exaggerated—so that those around him won't think what he already thinks about himself—that he's a borderline loser in some way.

Don't play this game. Most boys and men are irritated by a braggart or a show-off because he's constantly trying to dominate them with, "Oh, that's nothing. Do you know what I did?" It's a fast way to lose the respect of your friends.

Girls and women may be impressed momentarily by this guy but the shine wears off quickly when they realize he's mainly interested in himself.

The best way to show off your achievements is to simply be who you are. Those around you will come to know your manners, your intellect, your self-confidence, and your gifts fairly quickly. They will learn you are an amazing trumpet player, a successful businessman, an award-winning bowler, a decorated war hero, or maybe just a great friend.

Behavior

If you need to impress someone to win their favor, go ahead and tell them your good points. But if you find you are using your accomplishments to dominate the conversation or others, it's time to put it to bed.

Bragging can be a demonstration of weakness. Show off your strengths by having the self-discipline to not use your successes to undermine the self-confidence of others.

21. Don't pry into other people's business unnecessarily.

"Examples of behaviour that can undermine... trust and cohesion, and therefore damage the morale or discipline of a unit (and hence its operational effectiveness) include: Probing into a person's private life and relationships."

(British) Armed Forces Code of Social Conduct

At first look, this may not seem to have much to do with honor but it definitely is something that men expect of each other.

Prying into other people's business is a sort of predecessor to gossip. If you have no practical need for this information, then it implies that you are simply being nosy. It's an invasion of privacy.

Sometimes you have to look into a person's private life. You may think your neighbor has an illegal drug lab in his house. You may be concerned that your brother or sister has an addiction he or she needs help with. A parent's memory may be slipping and the electric bill isn't getting paid. One of your friends may be suicidally depressed and you want to save her life.

But if you just want to hear all the titillating details of Jill's abortion, Jim's gambling problem, Eric's salary, or Samantha's new boyfriend, just to satisfy your lurid curiosity, you need to recognize that you're putting your nose where it doesn't belong.

Like gossip, this is preying off of other people in their private moments. Also like gossip, prying into other people's affairs doesn't look good on a man. This is the business of tabloids and negative people. If you're a man of strength and honor, you don't need this to make your life satisfying.

Besides, you want to make the people around you feel safe. They won't if they think you are unnecessarily probing into their affairs. No one likes that and it will lower their faith in you. They will feel you cannot be trusted with private information because you will use it to dig up more.

22. Harm no one without good cause.

"Eschew unfairness, meanness and deceit."

Knight's Code of Chivalry

Throughout our lives men are called upon to fight. These battles take place on sports fields, in armored tanks, in courtrooms, and in bullies' neighborhoods around the world. We fight with our fists, our words, our minds, our strategies, our brawn—anything that will forward us to victory.

In these fights, we necessarily work to defeat our adversaries. In business, we crush the competition by winning a contract from them through a better sales presentation. On the battlefield, we mow down enemy combatants in a contest of life and death. At the school dance, we turn on our best charm to shine above the competition and win the heart of the girl of our dreams.

In competitive wars such as these, it is a man's duty to best his opponents. The pain you bring, of course, should be appropriate to the challenge. In a court case, for example, you want justice, not the ruination of your opponent. In combat, you wouldn't kill a man if he was willing to surrender.

Because men deal so much with force and emotional intensity, it is easy to misuse it. It's easy to lash out at someone who doesn't deserve it. It's easy to want vengeance, to jump to conclusions, to want to mete out justice NOW.

True justice, however, requires that we do not misuse our strength or positions of power to hurt those who don't deserve it. Don't shoot the messenger. Don't take a bad day out on your kids or wife. Don't fire someone without a fair hearing. And don't say hurtful things you will later regret.

Even with your emotions under control you can be in a position to harm an innocent person. Maybe you're jealous.

Perhaps you want someone to take the fall for your crime. It could be that you just have a mean streak.

Resist the temptation. As men, our higher nature posts us as guardians, not oppressors. We have an obligation to see that those around us are treated fairly. Making someone take a hit he doesn't deserve is not fair.

23. Use a firm handshake.

"Have the right handshake (no bone crunching or limp wristed efforts)."

Gentlemen's Code of Conduct

One of the quickest ways men size each other up is by our handshake. For most men, a firm handshake is a sign of a guy who has his wits about him and is sincere in greeting you. It also means he's not a wimp but has some energy and strength in his actions.

On the reverse side, a limp grasp tells you the fellow may have his head in the clouds, thinking of something else. Or he's afraid or nervous. Or he is weak muscularly or has a low drive and energy level. Certainly, he is not enthusiastic about meeting you. Whatever the reason, a dead-fish handshake from another guy turns most men off. It can literally lessen the bond between the two men when you'd think the guy offering his hand would want to increase that connection.

Behavior

Men tend to thrive around strong men. Men of power and strong will—be it physical, mental, or simple drive—raise the bar for the rest of us. They set a tough pace that brings out the best in us so that we can keep up with them. They work harder, longer, and make better money. Males inherently know that strong men make better friends, business partners, comrades-in-arms, and teammates.

The fastest way to communicate that you are one of those strong males is by a firm handshake. It says you're with the program. You are willing to put energy and focus into your meeting and whatever challenges follow. If you're shaking on a deal, it also means that you are sincere in your agreement and that you'll stick to it.

Some cultures outside the Western world may not expect a firm handshake amongst males, for reasons best known to them. Know the rules of the land when you're there. But in the Western Hemisphere a handshake should have meaning in it.

Of course, a guy can fake a strong handshake to look honest and frank. It's not a guarantee. But it's a great first step and gives at least a hope between men that they are dealing with a straight shooter who not only has a firm grip but a strong character.

24. Look a person in the eye when you greet him.

"Stand up straight and look your hearers in the face."

The Extension Workers' Code—1922

This goes right along with the firm handshake. Looking a person in the eye communicates presence and strength. It means that you can face him, man to man.

It means you have nothing to hide. You're not worried about what he'll see when he peers into your soul.

And it shows respect, that you are acknowledging his presence.

Couple that with a strong grip and you have the start of a conversation with vigor and focus on both sides.

In the Western hemisphere, this applies equally to your dealings with women. But be aware that this may not be approved in all cultures.

25. Do not let anger rule your conduct.

"Men are like steel. When they lose their temper,
they lose their worth."

Chuck Norris

With plenty of testosterone coursing through our veins, anger is an emotion with which men and boys are quite familiar. When things don't go our way, when frustration sets in, or when someone crosses us, most of us can be counted on to feel the fuming impulse.

While that reaction can be useful in some dangerous situations—such as someone hurting your child, your

Behavior

possessions or even yourself—anger has limited value. More often than not, when he gives into the fury that rises up inside, a man does more harm than good.

Wars, murder, brutality, fights, torture, destruction, vengeance that can go on for generations—this is the reckless chaos that anger brings.

We end up saying hurtful things. We make sudden, rash judgments and decisions. We hurt our friends and loved ones and ourselves with our cruel actions. Some men go to prison. In short, we end up with a lot of regrets. And we certainly don't feel honorable afterwards.

Even in situations of danger, such as when someone is threatening you or your family or if your military unit is under attack, keeping your cool is far better than letting your emotions rule. You need to respond sensibly and effectively in such circumstances, considering the consequences of your actions, not simply react in an unthinking tirade.

In war films, we see a soldier looking on in outrage as his best friend is shot and then leaping out of his foxhole, storming toward the enemy and mowing them all down in a hail of gunfire.

That's fiction. In real life, a smart soldier would not jump into the open on a suicide mission. If he really wanted revenge, he'd coolly consider how he could stay alive so he could take out as many of the enemy as possible.

One of the basic tasks all men face in life is to learn to control their tempers. For some guys who are real hotheads, it's a lot harder than others. It doesn't matter. You need to rein it in.

One action that will dramatically improve your control of your anger is to apologize to those you have hurt after it happens. Don't just sweep it under the rug or act like nothing happened. Face it. A man who answers up for his mistakes is less likely to keep making them.

26. Do not let your appetites rule you.

"He who reigns within himself and rules passions, desires, and fears is more than a king."

John Milton

Men are known for their appetites. Movies are loaded with scenes of the king's men feasting on food, gangsters downing mugs of beer and bottles of whiskey, and cowboys chasing women down at the saloon.

Our appetites can give us great pleasure in life. Unfortunately, they can also be our ruin.

Too much food or too much of the wrong kind of food can ruin our health and negatively affect our behavior. A seriously overweight man simply doesn't feel as good as he would if he were lighter, and this not only affects his performance as an employee, a husband, and a father, but it affects his moods. Too much junk food can make a guy feel lousy with fatigue, heartburn, and sluggishness.

Behavior

Too much alcohol—the list of disasters from this nasty habit is endless. If we just look at how it kills, we see many thousands dying yearly from alcoholism, alcohol-related vehicle accidents, and alcohol-related diseases like heart and liver failure.

Drugs are equally dangerous and can own a man's soul with cravings and despair.

The appetite for sex, a wonderful thing, can go out of control, leading to infidelity, the use of prostitution, rape, pornography addiction, and high-risk sex resulting in unwanted pregnancies and sexually-transmitted diseases.

Gambling is another popular guy sport. Whether it's horse races, poker night, or trips to the casino, it's a thrill that can quickly get out of hand.

Men are quite familiar with these temptations. If we haven't completely fallen prey to them (and we've all succumbed to some of them at some time), then we've known numerous men close to us who have.

Some males have addictive personalities and get hooked on things easily. For them, life can be one long battle until they learn to get the upper hand.

When your appetites rule you, you are at the hands of fate, watching yourself eat or drink or gamble yourself into negative states. There is no self-respect, no sense of honor—just a deep understanding that you are harming yourself and probably others—and worst of all, you are doing nothing to stop it. This is a dark pit to live in.

Make an effort to get a handle on your carnal and obsessive impulses. Don't let them own you.

4

COURAGE

A FEW YEARS ago, my wife came to me with tears in her eyes. She had just spoken to her father. He calmly informed her that he had been diagnosed with brain cancer and that he had a very limited time left. The news was sudden and unexpected.

After collecting herself, she told me how proud she was of him for his courage in this dark hour. I was struck by the fact that here was a man about to lose everything but who had managed to muster the strength to give his family a measure of what they needed most at the moment—peace of mind. He gave them no suffering or regrets to watch but casually enjoyed each day to the last.

During this period I had a lot of stress on my plate in business and other areas, and my wife would occasionally get an earful from me about my troubles. After watching my father-in-law's example, I realized that, while we can try our best, none of us is exempt from life's random punches. As the head male of my household, I could see that I had not been as strong as him. I need to take what comes with as much grace as possible. To do otherwise is to add my burden to others who already have their own crosses to bear.

27. Stand tall in the face of adversity.

"The ultimate measure of a man is not where he stands in moments of comfort and convenience, but where he stands at times of challenge and controversy."

Martin Luther King, Jr.

Mark Twain once observed, "Courage is resistance to fear, mastery of fear—not absence of fear."

All rational men have tasted fear and anxiety. Your car is skidding off the road. You get a letter from the IRS. You've lost your job. Your wife tells you she wants a divorce. You are about to walk into a combat zone.

Life is filled with danger of all kinds. For a twelve-year-old, it may be an assignment to give a speech in front of class. For a six-year-old, it could be his dad coming home when the boy knows he's in trouble for hurting his younger brother.

But for boys and men, worse than being afraid is having to face the fact that you are behaving like a coward. When we do that, we all know that we have stepped away from our basic duty as a male and, in our hearts, there will be no forgiveness for this.

That duty is to face life as it comes. We are protectors, guardians, and soldiers—or we are working toward taking on those roles. We are depended upon to show and exercise strength. This includes the fortitude it takes to push yourself front and center, confronting the problems of living.

When does fear become cowardice? When it causes you to back away from what you know you should do.

Let us examine courage and cowardice in some of the above examples.

With the letter from the IRS, the man who stands tall opens the letter, reads it, and deals with it. The coward throws it out or puts it on a pile of other unread mail, and if the IRS calls him, he says he never got it.

The man who lost his job tells his wife, if he's married, or whoever else should know. He then goes about finding another job or planning his next career move. The man who gives into his fears perhaps goes out and gets drunk and holes up in bed for the next few days feeling sorry for himself.

The man threatened with divorce rationally confronts his wife on the matter, tries to salvage his marriage or acknowledges that this is the end of the line. He deals with the consequences. The coward falls apart, screams at his wife and disappears for three days as if that will somehow solve the situation.

The boy with the speech does his homework and gathers the strength to stand before class and make his presentation, for better or worse. The fellow who gives in to fear fakes an illness the day of the speech.

We all feel fear, stress and anxiety. It's painful, sometimes terrifyingly or numbingly so. But running and hiding from life conjures constant fear in our hearts and minds as the objects of our terror pursue us. Facing our fears means having to step before them just once.

Stand tall in the face of adversity. You will not only save yourself from running from your fears. You won't have to run from the guilt in your heart either.

28. Do what needs to be done.

"Do what has to be done."

Code of the West (James Owen)

It's 3 AM. You're awakened from a sound sleep by a barking dog. You slowly realize it's your dog, and he's raising hell in your yard outside your neighbor's bedroom window. The last thing you want to do is deal with it. You want to go back to sleep. But if you do, your neighbor pays the price for something you are responsible for.

Get up and handle it.

You've put in a long day at work and get home after dark. You see that one of your wife's tires is low. It might be flat

Courage

by morning. Your impulse, of course, is to ignore it, go in the house and flop down on the couch with some eats. But that could cost your wife her life in an accident or leave her with a massive problem when she finds a flat tire in the morning.

Do what needs to be done.

Life is filled with urgencies of large and small matters. Some have minor consequences. Others must be dealt with to avoid damage, pain, major losses, or even catastrophe.

History has countless lessons from men who didn't act when they should have. The king who ignored an army advancing on his castle. The wealthy man who saw his business declining but carried on with his wild spending. The basketball coach with the star center who flaunts the rules without being disciplined, then suddenly doesn't show up for the big game.

One of the main reasons men don't want to deal with matters is because they don't know what to do, or they can't comprehend some or all of the factors involved. This causes a sense of confusion and indecision. Doing what needs to be done often means facing chaos, your own brain fog, or things you don't understand and forcing yourself to comprehend the situation as best as you can and act. No one likes this. When faced with the fog of noncomprehension, our natural tendency is to turn away and ignore.

You're a student and you've been handed an assignment that's over your head and it could cost you your grade. You're a mechanic and you just wrecked a customer's engine trying to fix something you've never seen before. Your girlfriend just informed you that she's pregnant.

This means reaching into your gut, focusing, setting aside what you'd rather do, and fixing the matter so it stays fixed.

Real men take responsibility for their lives and don't dump the consequences on their mothers, girlfriends, kids, employers, neighbors or comrades-in-arms.

Don't shove it off onto someone else. The buck stops with you. Do what needs to be done.

29. Defend yourself and your interests.

> "It is our duty still to endeavor to avoid war; but if it shall actually take place, no matter by whom brought on, we must defend ourselves. If our house be on fire, without inquiring whether it was fired from within or without, we must try to extinguish it."
>
> **Thomas Jefferson**

Few things look as unmanly as a guy who won't defend himself or protect his family or possessions.

We are defenders by nature. Eons ago families and groups concluded, quite rightly, that the men should be the ones sent out in battle. They are bigger, stronger, and less likely to be preyed upon as are women and children. They are also a little more dispensable, since the children left behind are usually more dependent on mothers for their immediate care. Men have traditionally looked out for the security of their homes, wives, children, and nations.

Even in play, boys have a strong tendency to reach for the weapons and military gear. If you were to ask a five-year-old boy who in his class he can beat up, most likely he can tell you in a heartbeat. He's already sized up the matter. It is the nature of being male.

Every boy and man will face countless situations in his life where someone attacks him or his interests. It could be attempted theft, a lawsuit, an assault on his reputation, an attempt to take his girlfriend, a punch in the face, a bad check, harm to his child, or any number of things.

It's an old law of the jungle: If you don't respond in self-defense, you encourage further aggression against you and yours. If you stand up and defend, you send the message that you are not an easy mark.

Of course, not every petty insult and annoyance requires a response from you. And a man doesn't have to be a tough guy 24/7 to defend what's his. He just needs to act when the situation calls for it.

30. Use force as a last resort, then use it well.

"Don't hit at all if it is honorably possible to avoid hitting; but never hit soft!"

Theodore Roosevelt

We've all heard of "girl fights." But no one uses the phrase "boy fight." That's because fighting is a given in the male realm.

Force and strength are part of the male DNA. We are commonly well-muscled, like contact sports, and almost every boy ends up in a few fistfights before he makes it out of high school. Boxing, wrestling, martial arts, weaponry—these are primarily our domain.

We have a fondness for force. Hollywood knows this. If you want men to watch, give them fights, car crashes, hard-hitting sports, military battles, action movies.

And we have a strong tendency to use force. Our body chemistry makes us quicker to anger and our primitive drives urge us to do physical damage when our tempers are aroused.

But human history is strewn with the wreckage of our spent rage. We've piled bodies high, razed cities and towns, and set back civilization repeatedly by our reckless brutality.

One of the greatest embarrassments of manhood is facing the consequences of our misuse of force. You might physically assault someone you think wronged you, only to find he was innocent. Or you spank your child severely before you stop yourself. Maybe you take a baseball bat to a guy's car after he runs into yours. Or in your anger, you slap your girlfriend.

It could just be that you like to yell a lot.

Courage

We all know the feeling after the fury has died down and we realize what we've done. Force is like any other power. It can be used for good or evil. It is the journey of every man to learn to channel his forceful urges constructively.

And as a defense, it must be used as a last resort, after reason and discussion have failed or when it becomes obvious that no other choice is possible. Otherwise, our lifespan becomes a trail of broken relationships and damage from our repeated blowups, and we may even come to feel so guilty that we are afraid to use force when we rightly should.

But when you must use it, use it well, within legal limits. As Theodore Roosevelt said, "Speak softly and carry a big stick." If you are called out in the schoolyard and you have no choice but to defend yourself..., if a man is trying to snatch your child..., if your wife's alcoholic brother decides to use her for a punching bag in front of you..., or if someone is shooting at you...

Fate has called on you. Now is when you bring the sword from your sheath and use it with extreme prejudice.

It may not even be physical force. It could be legal force like calling the police or filing a lawsuit or evicting someone from your property.

When the time comes for such events, you usually know. Use your power sparingly but don't falter at the trigger when the shot has to be fired and aim well.

31. Be prepared to risk you life or safety for a greater good.

"I am an American, fighting in the forces which guard my country and our way of life. I am prepared to give my life in their defense."

Military Code of Conduct

No boy or man wants to lose his life or health. It's perfectly normal to fear death or injury and to avoid it at all costs. But occasionally in life we face a crossroads, where we must choose, often quickly, between our own safety and that of a greater good.

What you choose at that moment is up to you. But as a man or boy, you must resign yourself to the fact that this moment will come, possibly numerous times in your life.

Many men who respond to such moments and become heroes often remark that they don't feel like heroes. "I didn't think about it," they commonly say. "I just felt I should do something and I did it."

You may be comfortably watching a ballgame on TV when you hear a child scream in the dark streets outside. Perhaps your generation's Pearl Harbor or 9/11 will unfold in front of you and your nation will call for your sacrifice on the battlefield. You could turn the corner and find a family trapped in a burning vehicle. Or maybe you're a young teen watching your father beat your mother.

Sometimes it's not even a greater good. It's simply an urgent matter, like a dog has fallen through the ice on a frozen lake.

A lot can go through your mind at that moment. Your kids need a father. Your wife needs a husband. Your parents need your support. Is it worth the risk? Or maybe nothing goes through your mind—some guys just act. But you will ultimately have to make that decision and live with the consequences.

Be prepared. Know that time will come when you will be called upon, often randomly, simply because you are the closest man to the situation. It's nothing personal. But when the dust clears, if you didn't act, people may ask why. After all, you are a man—a protector of society—and people inherently expect that it should have crossed your mind.

You may not be able to decide in advance. Who can know until that time comes? But you can at least settle with yourself that, as a male member of our society, your life and safety is not wholly yours. A time will likely arise when you will be asked to put them on the line for others.

32. Face death with courage.

"If I am killed, I can die but once; but to live in constant dread of it, is to die over and over again."

Abraham Lincoln

All of us will die. In fact, in our modern times, most of us will get a general idea of when we are going to die. These days people rarely drop dead from sudden illnesses. Even with strokes and heart attacks, most sufferers have some advance warning from their doctor that "the big one" might be coming.

The bottom line is that our lives will end. None of us want to die and nearly all of us fear death, but we must deal with it nonetheless.

Let's take a look at a man who doesn't want to contend with it. He's told he has six months to live. He's shocked and overwhelmed by the news. He cries in his car most of the way home, thinking about all that he is about to give up. When he gets home, he tells his wife the bad news. He tells her it's not right. He's too young. He doesn't want to leave her or the children.

Days go by and he continues to bemoan his bad fortune. As his health deteriorates, his fear becomes terror and he clings to his family at every turn until he no longer has the strength to hold onto the anxiety. Finally, exhausted and miserable, he slips into unconsciousness, then death.

Now let's look at a man who faces death with courage. He, too, may cry most of the way home, because courage doesn't mean you don't care or feel. But this man has a sense of honor. He sees himself as a source of strength, calm, and security for his family and friends. He also does not want to burden their lives unnecessarily—he has spent his entire life being a pillar of support and a force for good, not a burden.

Sick though he may be, he sees that his wife, children, family and friends will be the ones who will really suffer. Because they will have to live with his absence, a grieving process that can take years.

If he were to fall into self-pity, this would only add to their suffering. And for what? Just because he wouldn't face the inevitable?

This man also realizes that it is better to spend his final minutes, hours, and days enjoying what he has, rather than to languish in mental agony in a battle he will never win.

Of course, any sane man will fight like hell to dodge death, and that is just what he should do. Get a second or third medical opinion, vow to yourself you will not die as the medics drag you out of the range of gunfire, or keep putting one foot in front of the other if you are lost in a wilderness.

But whether you know for sure you will die or whether it is simply a strong possibility, meet death with courage. It may be the last manly act you give your family, the world, and yourself.

33. Always stand guard.

"The superior man, when resting in safety, does not forget that danger may come. When in a state of security he does not forget the possibility of ruin. When all is orderly, he does not forget that disorder may come. Thus his person is not endangered, and his States and all their clans are preserved.

Confucius

A long time ago, a columnist for an outdoors magazine wrote about an observation he had made during a camping trip. He noticed himself glancing about occasionally, looking at the hilltops, in the trees, along the ground. He realized he had seen other men do the same. It occurred to him that he was standing guard. He was scoping out potential dangers without thinking. Storm clouds, smoke, bears, rattlesnakes, strange voices: He instinctively looked and listened for dangers to his family, who were sleeping in a nearby tent.

Even in our civilized society, threats can come with little or no warning. If they are physical threats, the job of contending with them will usually fall to the man or men in the vicinity. If you are with your girlfriend, family, or female co-workers, then almost certainly the task will fall to you. This isn't to say that women can't defend themselves—sometimes better than men—but in the chaos of imminent danger, the usual instinctive response is to look to the most capable male or males to lead the charge.

So part of your role in life is to know this and watch for such threats. It doesn't mean you can never relax. It just means that your duties as a boy or man include keeping your eyes and ears open and knowing that you may have to respond swiftly.

5

WOMEN, CHILDREN, AND FAMILY

MANY YEARS AGO as I sat in my home, I heard the familiar slam of a car door in the driveway. My youngest daughter ran into the house panicked. "Mom needs your help!" she yelled.

I ran to find my wife, Betty—in her thirties then—struggling to stand up from the driver's seat. "Call 911, " she gasped. "I can't breathe." I ran into the house and made the call as my daughter looked at me fearfully.

By the time I got back to the car, Betty was flat on her back in the driveway and my oldest daughter, age thirteen, was administering CPR. I was stupefied. Nothing like this had ever happened before. I had no idea what I was witnessing. My wife of seventeen years, the love of my life, fought to breathe but no air came in or out. I knew this could not go on without terrible consequences.

I stepped in and continued the CPR. Each passing second was a jarring rope pulling my wife and best friend from me forever. I felt utterly helpless. Fortunately, we live two blocks from a fire station. After the longest few minutes of my life, paramedics arrived, administered emergency treatment, and took her to a nearby hospital.

We found out later that Betty had suffered from a severe allergic reaction called anaphylactic shock. Her throat had completely closed. But she made it and, thankfully, remains my life companion and the hearth of our home.

In my driveway that night, I had to face a feeling of utter despair as the clock ticked on. I might not be able to protect my wife and family. I realized that, had my daughter not started CPR, I may have been so dumbfounded that I would not have thought to do so myself. This was not the type of medical emergency for which I'd learned CPR. When the dust had settled and we learned that Betty's life had been spared with only seconds remaining, I was left to reflect on my fumbling efforts when so much was at stake.

I learned that one of the ways to measure a man's drive to protect the women and children in his midst is to have him consider how he would feel if he failed to do so.

34. Honor women and their feminine nature.

"Respect women."

Code of Chivalry

"Honor women and their feminine nature" is nearly a direct quote from The Knight's Code.

One of our greatest flaws as humans comes from our inclination to criticize and find fault.

Men commonly complain that women are too emotional, they shop too much, they cry easily, they're unpredictable, they worry too much about their appearance—and the list goes on.

But what men are really saying in most instances is that they love these qualities in women, except when it doesn't benefit the man.

We love their emotional nature when they rush to nurse our wounds. We can't get enough of it when they fall in love with us and tell us how they feel about us. And it's their exuberant voice we listen for in the stands when we step up to bat.

The same with shopping. We think differently when they bring home our favorite foods or pick up a tool we've been needing because they saw it on sale. And we don't mind so much when she buys that slinky red dress.

Let's face it, guys. Women are beautiful.

And contrary to our sweaty, gritty, muscling, hard-charging lives, the feminine gender can be soft, gentle, comforting, and nurturing—and sometimes they smell really good.

They melt us with their charms and, frankly, historically we have killed for them and over them many, many times because we value them so highly.

They are the keepers of our children. They turn our house or apartment, rich or humble, into a home. They capture our hearts and souls with their eyes, smiles, and laughter. And if we are lucky enough, they stand beside us as lifelong mates and lovers to help us in the battle to provide, raise a family, and find happiness in a tough world.

Of course, they are feminine. They have menstrual cycles so they can have babies. That's why we all have mothers and why we can be proud fathers. That's why they are hardwired to lavish all that maternal care on us. That's why they have estrogen and other hormones designed to drive our body chemistry wild.

Seriously, would you have it any other way?

This doesn't mean that women don't have faults or can't make a man miserable. All of us are flawed.

But if we are willing to pick up our swords to fight for them, it is only right that we be honest with ourselves about why we do this.

They bear our children, they are the foundation of our families. By and large, they are incredibly tolerant of our manly ways. And when we stand in good stead with them, they bring us heaven on earth.

They are the oasis in the deserts we cross.

Life is dull and gray indeed without them.
Honor women. And their beautiful, feminine nature.

35. Never use force against a woman except in self defense.

"One should never strike a woman; not even with a flower."

Hindu proverb

"Never hit a woman."

Virtually every boy and man in the Western world has been given that instruction at some time in his life. The reasons are obvious. Men are generally larger and stronger than women. In most cultures, the ultimate in respected male behavior is the "gentleman," and gentlemen treat women with deference, opening doors for them, offering them a seat, giving a woman their umbrella in the rain, etc.

Hitting a woman also goes against the very nature of a man's basic duties. We are protectors. What kind of protector commits violence against those in his charge?

Striking a female is considered completely unacceptable behavior by most men. If you don't believe it, just put a bunch of men in a room who have never watched female boxing for the first time. The gasps and moans will go on for minutes before they can get used to the idea of seeing a woman get hit in the face. It turns the average man's stomach.

Many a mild-mannered fellow has leaped to his feet upon hearing or witnessing a woman being battered. It can bring out the tiger in a man.

Some Eastern cultures, operating from dictates of centuries past, still permit violence against women. But these patterns are changing as equal rights for women become the norm in our modern world.

However, a man has every right to defend himself and others if a woman is violent or committing an act that has to be stopped. There are plenty of crimes of passion by women, and every guy should protect himself against physical assault, be it a knife, a fist, or a frying pan.

And "self-defense" includes defense of one's environment. If a woman is setting a fire, beating a child, pulling a gun on your friend…you may need to step in with a heavy hand.

But when it's simply a matter of tempers flaring—when she drives you so nuts you feel your fists clenching—it's time to take a walk.

This has to be a lifetime commitment for all men. Never hit a woman except in self defense.

36. Never force sex on anyone.

"If at any time you meet with a prudent Woman,
that Man that offers to meddle with her, without her
Consent, shall suffer present Death."

The Articles of John Philips, captain of the pirate ship Revenge

Women, Children and Family

The sexual urge exists throughout the animal kingdom. It has to if each of the species is to survive. Male and female are attracted to each other and driven to mate to ensure that the race continues.

In the human world, the more intense sexual drive is usually associated with males. Terms like rapist, registered sex offender, child molester—these normally refer to men.

This doesn't mean that all men are sexual predators—not by a long shot. But all men know that we are tainted by the acts of a minority who are. We all know that if we are walking down a dark street behind a woman that we can expect her to glance nervously over her shoulder or quicken her step. We know to keep our distance. And we know that if we have consensual sex with a woman and she cries "rape" that there is a great likelihood we will be presumed guilty rather than innocent.

From a young age, boys learn that we carry this mark of Cain upon our heads.

Moreover, we learn quickly that women generally do not face nearly the same penalties for the same crimes.

But there is good reason for all this. Forced sex on a woman bears a much stronger social stigma. It generally does more damage to her psyche. (This is not to say that it can't be traumatic for males.) There is always the risk of pregnancy. And commonly, violence or the threat of it accompanies forced sex by a male, leaving more trauma—sometimes for life—and possibly injuries to deal with.

Don't be a part of this.

The male sexual drive can be a powerful constructive force. It's one of the several biochemical lightning bolts that sizzle through our veins and prompt us to flex our muscles and stand with chests out like proud lions on battlefields, oil fields, and soccer fields. It leads us to swim shark-infested waters for our women and write amazing love songs and poetry. Properly channeled, it can provide a lifetime of pleasure with a loving, caring partner.

Misused, it violates our most primeval duty: to protect women and children.

Which brings us to our next tenet of the code...

37. Protect women and children.

"Never give evil counsel to a lady, whether married or not; [a knight] must treat her with great respect and defend her against all."

Oath of Knighthood

"No man stands so tall as when he stoops to help a child."

Abraham Lincoln

Men learn early in life, first subtly, then clearly, that their lives are more expendable than a woman or child's.

Women, Children and Family

We watch movies of ships sinking and hear, "Women and children first." We hear of policemen dying in the line of duty. We watch male soldiers get killed and maimed by the dozens and hundreds in war movies and military footage. Bodyguards, firemen, mercenaries, bomb squads—you name it. If it involves putting your life on the line in the defense of life and property, the job is usually done by a man.

And as we get older, we come to realize this is rightly so. While not all of us are born heroes and most of us don't want to be in harm's way, men do not complain about this arrangement. We understand that's the way it should be.

Our children—or kids in general—have their entire lives ahead of them. And we inherently know we must protect them. If they are our own children, there is no question that we must. But even kids who are not our own blood become immediate targets of rescue in a burning building, war zone, crime scene, or other dangerous situation.

And children, of course, need mothers. So women must be protected as well. Because they are, in general, physically smaller and weaker than men, it falls upon the males to protect the females when the going gets rough.

This doesn't mean that many a woman can't or won't defend herself or do some heavy lifting.

But it does mean that when danger strikes and the final decision has to be made, it falls upon men to protect the women and children in their midst.

38. Do not use crude language in the presence of children.

"Profanity around my house? No...I'm a parent, I have daughters...I mean how would I really sound, as a person, walking around my house [using profanity]...You know what I mean? I don't cuss."

Eminem

This is part of the previous tenet. Protecting children includes protecting their innocence. This means shielding them from corrupting influences like alcohol, pornography, tobacco and, yes, adult language.

Men can be quite free with foul language. Some don't even recognize it as such. It's just the way many of them talk. But, amazingly, most will catch themselves in the act around a child and stop because they don't want to hurt the young one by exposing him or her to profanity.

The innocence of childhood is much more short-lived in our modern world. Kids see things on TV and in movies and in real life that were hidden from their view only a generation before. But still it is the duty of all of us to let them have that innocence for as long as it will last. Children can detect that there is something not-quite-right about such speech and this can weigh upon them.

Cursing, using sexual or similar crude language can be a negative influence on a child's world.

Women, Children and Family

When does a child become old enough for such things? That's a cultural matter. Many adults in our society choose to use foul language rarely or not at all. Others may do so as a child enters his teens or when he has graduated into the adult world. Again, it is dependent on the views of the child's family and culture.

39. Do not use crude language in the presence of women without their approval.

"Don't swear or use offensive language in the wrong company."

Gentleman's Code of Conduct

Not so long ago, the tenet most men followed was: Don't curse in the presence of women—period.

And for many men, that viewpoint remains today. Religious men, for example, are often appalled at the idea of cursing in front of women. This stance is a form of honoring women and a simple matter of respect for the more wholesome side of life that they have historically represented.

But our culture has changed. While using foul language may still not be "ladylike," for better or worse, it has become more commonplace to hear such speech from females, or at least some forms of it.

For some women, to refuse to use such language around them makes them feel left out of the conversation. In fact, they may originate discussion on sexual matters or the use of profanity.

A reasonable rule of thumb would be to watch your tongue unless a woman has clearly shown you through her verbal cues or otherwise that she uses such language.

You may still choose to show respect and some class by avoiding cursing or crude talk. That's your call.

40. Always be faithful to your romantic partner.

"Thou shalt never lie, and shall remain faithful to thy pledged word."

Ten Commandments of the Code of Chivalry

A study done near the time of this writing found that 22% of married men and 15% of married women report cheating on their spouses. Other research finds similar results—depending on what you call cheating—with men normally offending more than females.

Like the rapist and wife-beater, the unfaithful man has done considerable damage to the reputation of men in general.

All men and boys have heard the accusations. "Men are pigs (or dogs)(or animals)." "Men just want one thing."

But the statistics you don't hear reported are the positive ones. If 22% of married men are unfaithful, that means that 78% are loyal to their marriage vows.

This tells us that most men are not "pigs." They take their marriage vows seriously, despite the many temptations in our world.

The building block of our society is the family. And the glue of the family is fidelity between spouses.

Cheating on your girlfriend, fiancé, or wife is one of the most treacherous things a boy or man can do. The damage done is immediate and deep and some partners never recover from it. If you manage to hide it, pity you because it will eat you alive and change you and your relationships for the worse.

Sometimes you hear guys make excuses for this. "My wife doesn't understand me." "No harm done if she doesn't find out." "It's not really cheating." "Other guys do it." These guys are a disgrace to the male gender. There's nothing cool or admirable about their actions. No matter how much power or money they have, they are losers. And any man who breaks his word to his wife or girlfriend will also lie to you and anyone else.

This is another line in the sand that all males must draw in their lives. If you want to be a real man, there are no exceptions and no excuses. Always be faithful to your romantic partner.

41. Never steal another man's romantic partner.

> "Examples of behaviour that can undermine...trust
> and cohesion, and therefore damage the morale

or discipline of a unit (and hence its operational effectiveness) include...over-familiarity with the spouses, civil partners or partners of other Service personnel...displays of affection which might cause offence to others...behaviour which damages or puts at risk the marriage, civil partnership or personal relationships of Service personnel or civilian colleagues within the wider defence community."

(British) Armed Forces Code of Social Conduct

Men can be very competitive. We fight each other for gains on the football field, in business, in politics, and even in the realm of romance. But when we compete, we have rules and an understanding amongst each other. And men don't respect other men who don't play by the rules.

One of those basic rules is that you never steal another man's girlfriend or wife. If a girl or woman is committed to another guy, you don't try to win her affections. You don't flirt with her. You don't seduce her with your charms, whatever they may be.

Men have killed over this—many, many, many times. It's not a small matter.

You have a friend in the service who is on duty in another country. He's left a wife at home whom he married shortly before going overseas. A few months go by and you figure she's an easy mark. She's lonely. Her husband is away. No one will know.

To steal a man's wife or girlfriend like that is not honorable. It shows that you do not respect commitment or the agreements of others. It means you will likely not respect your own promises when you are committed in a marriage or relationship.

Additionally, you'll make your own hell. We often see the world as a reflection of our own thinking. If you steal another man's partner, then you will always be wondering if another man will do the same to you.

Don't start up a relationship with a girl or woman who is "attached." If she is in the midst of a breakup or divorce, make sure the separation is final before you become romantically involved.

To do otherwise is to steal another man's partner.

42. Meet the romantic needs of your partner.

"If you would be loved, love and be lovable."

Benjamin Franklin

On the surface, this may seem like a touchy-feely matter that really should not be part of the Men's Code of Honor. Oh, but it is.

If you want to see an embarrassed and devastated man—one who has lost his sense of masculinity—find one who cannot meet the sexual needs of his partner.

Our airwaves are filled with commercials for drugs to help men with "erectile dysfunction." Billions of dollars worth of these medications are sold annually to tens of millions of men in the United States alone. Why? Because virility is one of the hallmarks of being a man. It is so important to us, we literally refer to our genitals as our "manhood." While it is normal to lose some virility with age, it is generally very upsetting to men when this happens to them.

What is virility? Merriam-Webster defines it as "having the nature, properties, or qualities of an adult male; specifically: capable of functioning as a male in copulation."

We are hardwired to procreate. It partly defines us as males. Many women do not want a man who can't have children. In most cultures, this makes a man a poor marriage candidate unless the couple is past the age of childbearing.

And most women would not marry a man who can't have sex for obvious reasons.

So—even though a lack of sexual function happens to most men at various times of life—men know on a primitive level that our virility defines us. Without it, we are not quite "real men."

On a strictly selfish level, a man who can meet the sexual needs of his partner is generally a more content man because he is fulfilling his biological imperative.

Additionally, we are hardwired to respond to receptive females because this, too, ensures procreation. Thus, when your partner is looking for romance and sending you signals, it is natural for you to want to make her happy.

However, we are not strictly biological beings. We also have the power to reason and observe. One of those observations is that a woman's romantic needs go beyond sex. They also like kisses, cuddling, compliments, gifts, a night on the town, and all kinds of things that make them feel loved, attractive, warm and fuzzy, and, well, womanly.

Many a man measures his manliness by his ability to meet those needs. There is a great satisfaction in it that gives a man a sense of wholeness.

Of course, some women may want things that are beyond a man's capacity to give such as expensive gifts, excessive physical demands, or extreme expectations on their partner's time. This may mean the couple is not compatible or the woman is unreasonable. Either way, a man should recognize this as a recipe for unhappiness, because he will be unable to accomplish a dictate that is deep in his genes—to fulfill his partner's needs.

Unfortunately, not all men are concerned about their partner's needs. These are usually selfish men who are not very empathetic about others in general. Their lack of concern costs them in life. Their partners suffer and they, as men, do not know the satisfaction of making their wives or girlfriends happy.

43. Love and support children.

"Children are the seeds of our future. Plant love in their hearts and water them with wisdom and life's lessons. When they are grown, give them space to grow."

Native American Code of Ethics

Our world can be a tough place for a child. Even in our richest nations, we find poverty, alcoholism and drug abuse, domestic violence, child abuse, ignorance, and a host of other things that make a child's world dangerous.

Given love, support, decent food, education and a safe environment, most kids will grow up to be happy, productive people. But without these things, they risk becoming criminals, burdens to society, social outcasts, or not growing up at all.

As men, we are programmed to make babies. That's a given. We are also programmed—most of us, at least—to provide for them. One of the most dramatic changes from boyhood to manhood happens when a man becomes a father. For many, this is a near-religious experience where we become focused like a laser beam on fulfilling the needs of our child and providing for our family. Our priorities have been intensely redefined. The selfishness and immaturity of youth is cast off, and we step forth a man willing to work night and day in the pouring rain to bring a paycheck home to his wife and child.

Women, Children and Family

Part of providing for your children is giving them love and support. Men differ on how they do this but for most it is their natural desire. They would be heartbroken if they were prevented from carrying it out.

But not all children in a man's life are his biological offspring. He could marry a woman who already has children. He could have younger siblings, cousins, neighbors, or he could be a teacher. These children also need a man's love and support.

When we raise our own kids, we do so with an understanding that we have a responsibility to them and to society to rear children who will be law-abiding citizens who will contribute to that society.

With other children, we have the same duties. We want to do those things that will help these children be happy, constructive individuals. We accomplish this by giving them love, support, guidance, tolerance, and by giving them an example of what proper adult conduct looks like.

44. Provide for your family.

"I will put my family first; before friends, community and even self. I will love, protect and provide for my family."

Native American Men's Code of Conduct

If you want to make a man feel utterly degraded, take away his ability to provide for his family.

Most men, upon finding they will become a father, are programmed to kick into high gear to provide for their young one, and that fire in the belly stays with them till the day they die.

However, many men are faced with a severe reality adjustment. They find that, biologically, it's very easy—even pleasurable—to become a father, but being a dad requires more of them than they think they can give.

These men—or boys—may be too young to be real dads. They could have substance abuse issues. They could be unemployed without job skills, uneducated, unwilling to change a bad lifestyle, unwilling to leave school, or immature. If so, they have committed one of the worst crimes a man can be involved in. They have brought a helpless living, breathing baby into the world without making absolutely certain that child will be provided for.

This child has no real father. In days of old, such a child could have been eaten by wild animals or left to starve. In modern society, we call it a single-parent family (assuming the mother is doing her job).

The wolves that will eat this child now are much slower in their task but just as deadly. Statistics show that children from fatherless homes have dramatically higher rates of suicide, running away, dropping out of high school, imprisonment, substance abuse, conviction for violent rape, behavior problems, physical and mental health problems, and teenage pregnancy.

All this because men did not stand tall and provide for their families.

To put a child and its mother through this misery and to burden society with your responsibility is one of the worst acts a man can commit.

Do not father children you cannot raise.

If you do have a child, ensure you man up and do what millions of years of biological refinement have built you to do—provide for your family.

45. Serve your young children's needs before your own.

"Let the children first be filled."

Jesus Christ, Mark 7:27

One of our primeval duties as fathers is to ensure the survival of our children, even if it means bringing discomfort to ourselves. This guarantees that our children reach adulthood and the family line and the race are continued.

When children are young, they are unable to fend for themselves, so need more assistance than adults. Also, adults have a much greater tolerance for stress so when some sacrifice is needed, it is the dad's duty to pay the price instead of burdening the child.

On a basic level, your family may be short on food. In this case, the child's needs supersede your own. He or she must be fed first. The same is true if there is a scarcity of water or other fluids.

Let's talk sleep. Babies or young children sometimes wake up in the middle of the night with nightmares, illnesses, or other needs. You may need to give up part or all of your precious night's rest to help your child. In extreme cases, this can go on for several nights in a row or much longer.

A father is also often faced with the dilemma of wanting to spend money on himself when his young kids have more pressing needs. You want a new sound system in your car but the kids need shoes. Serve your children's needs first. Their comfort is more important that yours.

At some point, as children become more self-sufficient and able to tolerate the stress of not having their needs fulfilled, the family's priorities may change. Cultures and families vary on when that shift occurs.

But when children are young and they need your resources, give them.

46. Marry the mother of your children.

"Love is an ideal thing, marriage a real thing."

Johann Wolfgang von Goethe

As of this writing, four in ten of America's children are born out of wedlock. It has become common for a man not to marry the mother of his children. Men or boys want to enjoy the pleasures of sex with females, but many don't want to take responsibility for the consequences of their actions if a child is conceived.

As a result, we get scenarios that bring sadness all around. Girls or women are left to raise a child on their own. Grandparents or other family members have to take on the lifetime commitment of caring for someone else's child. Kids grow up without fathers. Some grow up without mothers. Or perhaps the dad stays around but he doesn't want to marry the mother. He wants the benefits of marriage but he doesn't want the responsibilities. He likes the option of being able to walk away whenever he feels like it.

This has become so common that people speak of it as if it were just another lifestyle. It's not. It's a universal tragedy of horrific proportions. The kids and society pay a high price for this reckless behavior as we have seen.

And let's not forget men's dirty little secret that goes along with this: abortion. "Just get an abortion," so many men will say, as though it were the same as stepping on a bug. While abortion may be legal and scholars debate endlessly whether life begins at conception, one thing is for sure: For many women, *motherhood* begins at conception. They feel different with this new life inside them and they like it, and they want to fulfill their biological destiny and give birth to this baby, whether it's practical or not.

For many other women, this moment happens when they do a pregnancy test and find they are with child. Their own hardwiring kicks in and they realize, "I am a mom." Hormonal and other physical changes occur and the powerful instinct to protect their child goes into gear. They do not want to abort and no amount of reasoning will overcome their mother-bear instincts.

These women, pressured by boyfriends or casual sex partners to get an abortion, often go into a deep depression or drown in guilt for months or even years afterwards, feeling they have violated their most basic survival impulse: to protect their child. As a result, some of the most passionate advocates of the pro-life movement are women who have had abortions, women who have come to learn the unforgiving pain that can accompany this action.

Not all women feel this way, but you'll never know, will you? It doesn't matter if you or your girlfriend are "pro-life" or "pro-choice." You'll never know ahead of time if the girl or woman you impregnate and pressure to get an abortion will suffer, or even commit suicide, over the pain that she can't make go away.

Many men go through guilt over abortion as well, particularly when they later have a child. Then they see what it is they aborted and reality hits them hard.

So don't assume that abortion is a simple backup plan for your careless sexual habits. It's nowhere near as easy as it looks.

And how about the single moms who do decide to give birth? Approximately 37% live below the poverty line. Nearly half work more than one job. The average income of a single mother with a child under six is one quarter that of a comparable two-parent family. These girls and women commonly have to give up sleep, personal time, and household chores just to get a few minutes with their kids. They suffer more health problems, have the highest rate of unemployment and receive the lowest rate of pay, despite their education.

In an extensive study of children born out of wedlock, the Brookings Institute, one of America's leading think tanks, stated in their report, "Strengthening Fragile Families," that "nonmarital" births are "assuring the persistence of poverty, wasting human potential, and raising government spending."

"The most important conclusion," they said, "is that these families play a central role in boosting the nation's poverty rate and that they and their children contribute disproportionately to many other serious social problems."

A recent report to Congress by the U.S. Department of Health and Human Services is crystal clear on why a man should marry the mother of his children: "Compared to children living with married biological parents, those whose single parent had a live-in partner had more than 8 times the rate of maltreatment overall, over 10 times the rate of abuse, and nearly 8 times the rate of neglect."

So what kind of a man would do that to a woman—leave her with a child and put her in a position where she labors ceaselessly for years, constantly strapped for money, gives up her dreams and opportunities, and suffers ill health from the stress and sacrifice?

What kind of a man would force a child to endure these same hardships and grow up without the guidance and love of a father and put this kid at risk of becoming a gang member, pregnant teen, high school dropout, criminal, or simply someone with a bleak future?

And what kind of a man refuses to marry the mother of his children so that he can avoid the legal and moral consequences of marriage?

Marry the mother of your children. Make that your personal policy. Set the bar that high for yourself. It will make you think twice about reckless behavior and a casual night of sex. It will cause you to select your partner wisely.

Men who don't set the bar that high are willing to put girls, women, and children through hell to pay for their irresponsibility. These are not honorable men.

Marry the mother of your children.

47. Make your home a sanctuary of security for your family.

"I will work to make my home a place of safety and security for my family—A Sanctuary."

Native American Men's Code of Conduct

Women, Children and Family

Men are guardians by nature so one of our most natural functions is to preserve the sanctity and peace of our homes. Our wives and children need safety and a sense of ease if they are to be able to relax at home, away from the stresses of work, school, troublesome relatives, or a thousand other things. We, too, need our rest and a place of sanctuary where we can recuperate from the day's labors and carry on our hobbies, household chores, or downtime.

The great irony of this, however, is that other parts of our makeup can cause us to be the source of the very violence or chaos that we, by nature, want to keep out of our homes.

There's that famous temper, alcohol abuse, or allowing disturbing friends or family members into your home. There's yelling, cursing, undisciplined children, and spousal arguments.

So one of the first orders of business is to ensure that you are not violating the peace of your home. Then ensure all other household members are working with you toward this same goal. That includes the famous warning virtually every child with two parents has heard: "Wait till your father gets home."

Beyond that, there is the need to protect against intruders. People have different views on how to do this, depending upon where they live, the security of their neighborhood, and what they believe. It could be a gun, a good fence, good outside lighting, a locked gate, an alarm system, or other approaches.

And of course, let's not forget about natural enemies. Rats, bugs, spiders, snakes, raccoons, and lots of other pests can invade your house and threaten your family and property. As the family protector, it is your job to ensure your family is safe. Do it.

48. Do not unnecessarily burden your family.

"I don't want to be a burden on my family. I need to live life."

Jack LaLanne

Given a man's natural inclination to provide for and protect his family, the last thing he wants to do is become a burden for them. We see this in men who become seriously ill or injured or crippled. They commonly go into a deep depression because they are no longer able to carry out their manly functions. The thought of forcing their wives to take an extra job or their children to suffer because of want can be intolerable.

For some men, this is an unavoidable consequence of life. Perhaps a motorcycle accident has left him in a wheelchair. He could have suffered a traumatic brain injury in war. Through no fault of his own, he could have inherited a debilitating illness.

Women, Children and Family

For these men, the process of coming to grips with the situation can be a slow and painful one. They search their souls for answers and reconcile themselves to the situation as best as they can. If they are lucky, they may be able to work around their disability so they can still earn a paycheck.

There's no dishonor in such misfortune. Many good men are brought to their knees by tragedy and do their best with what they've got.

But what about the man who brings on his own misfortune? We're talking about the gambler, the heavy drinker, the compulsive eater, the reckless athlete, the drug abuser. And we're talking about the lazy bum, the know-it-all with lousy financial judgment, the dangerous driver, the womanizer, and the cocky guy who ignores all safety precautions.

These are preventable tragedies. But they are only prevented if a man realizes that his actions can and likely will bring financial or emotional damage to his family.

Throughout his life a man has to periodically take an inventory of his habits and behaviors to weed out those that have become threats to his and/or his family's wellbeing. Perhaps your overeating was not a big deal when you got married, but now you're over 300 pounds, and you can't run with your kids, and your health problems threaten to keep you from working.

You may have been able to blow a week's pay at the casinos when you were single but now you have kids to feed and there's no room in the budget for a missing paycheck.

Do not unnecessarily burden your family. They need you.

49. Don't make your mother cry.

"I saw how, when my brother smoked reefer, it made my mother cry. He was 16 at the time. And I saw that she broke down and cried. I never wanted to hurt my mother, so I kept away from drugs."

Ving Rhames

Of all the tenets of the Men's Code of Honor, this is the only one that is simply a self-evident rule. You won't find it in traditional codes for men.

Yet any man or boy knows this rule, even if we don't know why. It just makes us feel awful if we make our mothers cry.

Amongst a group of men, if one were to knowingly bring his mother to tears, the remaining males would generally be seriously upset with this guy.

Of course, a few rare women use tears deliberately to get their children's attention, and boys who grow up with these mothers can become numb to the concept.

But generally mothers try not to burden their children so when the tears come out, we know we've really gone too far.

Women, Children and Family

50. Plan and prepare for your family's future.

"Plan for the future because that's where you are going to spend the rest of your life."

Mark Twain

A husband is responsible for the survival of his family. His wife can earn more than him. He may even have a happy arrangement with his wife for him to stay at home while she works. His wife could be a professional financial planner. But this doesn't free him from the obligation of ensuring his family has a secure future. There is no, "Hey, it's not my fault. I thought my wife was supposed to take care of that."

Planning for the future includes a lot of possibilities. It can mean buying a house, having health and life insurance, planning for your kids' college. It includes investments and educating yourself or your spouse for career advancement.

People differ on how much they invest in their future and their children's future, but some planning is required if you want to survive and even more planning is needed if you wish to prosper and improve your quality of life.

Not all men are math wizards or financial geniuses. Some can't organize a toolbox, much less their family's future. Often their spouses may be better at keeping a budget and buying stocks or insurance. That's fine. Part of intelligent decision-making is knowing when to choose someone more competent than you to ensure something gets done properly.

Just make sure it gets done. Don't reach your forties, fifties, and sixties, telling your wife and kids, "I should have..." It could be too late then.

51. Support actions that make a better world for our children.

"It's up to each of us to help create a better world for our children."

Dr. Benjamin Spock

This is simply an extension of protecting your children.

A lot of people have no interest in politics or what goes on in the neighborhood. They don't think about pollution, the nation's future, the drug dealer on the corner.

For most men, that changes after they have children. Suddenly, the world you've been ignoring is the environment your children have to live in. They have to breathe the dirty air, walk past gang members on their way to school, or listen to the neighbor's daily foul language as he screams at his dog.

Suddenly, it is your children who will have to sacrifice to pay the nation's debt, struggle to find a job in a tough economy, and fight the wars the country becomes entangled in.

A well-known law of physics tells us: All things tend toward entropy (chaos or randomness). This means everything, left on its own, has a tendency to decay. The world is a wonderful example of this. Houses need regular repairs, paint peels, countries rise and fall, and economies thrive and fail. In other words, it is natural for the world to come apart before our very eyes—unless acted upon by an outside force.

That outside force is you and the many others who work to keep order in our world.

Regardless of your politics, there are many ways to measure the events around you. A primary one is: Do they make a better world for our children? If not, act accordingly.

6

WORK

By the time I reached adolescence, my father had spent most of my lifetime in mental hospitals. During one particular period in my early teens when he was home, I heard him tell my mother he had managed to get a job. She was furious, telling him the family would make more money on welfare than from his minimum-wage labors. My father, troubled though he was, could not conceive of avoiding work to support his family if he had the ability and opportunity to do so. He also could not imagine himself collecting welfare if he was fit enough to work.

I saw him come home from his job at a factory that manufactured "sweeping compound," a red sawdust product that smelled like gasoline, used as an aid to cleaning floors. Dad stepped off the bus at the end of the day, his clothes stained red and reeking of petroleum.

Not long after, he got a job shoveling scrap wire into an industrial oven that burned the insulation off the metal. It was the only work he could find, a two-hour bus ride to and from our home. When I asked him about what he did, he talked with pride about how hard he worked all day to do his job well.

I was ashamed of him in those days. I didn't want my friends to know about his mental condition and humble occupation. But as I look back, I see what my youthful eyes did not—that I also held this man in awe. I could not then imagine myself enduring what he did—forcing himself to rise at 4 AM every day to face riding buses for four hours, toxic fumes, scratches from jagged metal, back-breaking shoveling, the blast of a furnace, and working in filth on a daily basis. And still, he took pride in his labor and took seriously his duty to earn his pay.

Decades later, as I look upon these things, my father embarrasses me for a different reason. I'm not so sure I would have stood as tall in his shoes.

52. Take pride in your work.

"Take pride in your work."

Code of the West (James Owen)

One of the attributes men admire most about other men is their craftsmanship, their ability to do their jobs. It's common to see men stop and stare at a busy construction

Work

site. We love to watch cops solve a mystery, a football player who runs like a gazelle, a carpenter constructing a staircase, or a chef cooking up an exquisite meal.

Why? We love competence. It is practically an art form amongst men. We watch a lumberjack work a saw or a crane operator hit his mark as though we were witnessing a ballet or symphony. As individuals, of course, we may tend to admire such excellence only in certain fields, but we love it nonetheless.

Competence means you have the ability to do or make something of value. That makes you valuable. And that means survival. It means you are an attractive mate, that you can make a living and provide for yousrself and your family. It means that you may have other survival skills like the ability to build a house, fix cars, work financial deals, farm, or cook. It's also a sign that you may have survival traits like intelligence, focus, persistence, dexterity, stamina, creativity and strength.

Boys are always in awe of the confident man who knows his trade. They want to be that way when they grow up. They want to be the veterinarian who accurately diagnoses a dog's illness and restores him to life, bringing joy to its owner. They want to be the bus driver who works his route with ease without an accident.

Men who don't know their jobs feel insecure to some degree. They know they are not as good as the pros in their field. They lack knowledge or experience. That may be perfectly acceptable if they are just learning the trade, but if they've been at it for a while, they know in their hearts they are second-rate.

Most jobs aren't glamorous. Some can be quite tedious. You may work in a factory punching holes in plastic all day to make toys. You may be a bill collector calling unwilling debtors on a daily basis. But whatever your line of work, you can do it in a competent fashion. That makes you more valuable to yourself, your family and your employer. That means better job security, possibly more pay, and likely, a better future.

Competence involves learning your trade. It requires practice and knowing your tools and using the right ones correctly. It may mean furthering your education in your field or keeping up with developments in your industry. It may even be wise to belong to a trade association or guild that specializes in your work.

Unless you have a very simple job, few become experts overnight. Most boys and young men want the rewards of being a professional before they've spent the time to become one. To make up for their lack of skill, they may even brag about being better than they really are. Patience is not usually a virtue of the young. But patient you must be.

What about work outside of your job? What about the home repairs, washing the car, sweeping the driveway, or raking leaves? The same rule applies for the same reasons.

Take pride in your work. Do it well. Others are depending on you to do so, whether it is your co-workers, your customers, or those expecting you to bring home a paycheck. A job well done brings a sense of pride and is one of the important roads that lead to an honorable life.

53. Don't be lazy.

"Anyone being lazy or failing to clean his weapons will lose their share of booty."

Pirate Code of Conduct

"Lazy" is defined as unwilling to work or use energy, a lack of desire to expend effort.

Every boy and man has had to carry an extra load because of some guy's laziness. This is the fellow who wants to goof off when the boss isn't around. He calls his girlfriend, wastes time on the computer, sits on the ground smoking a cigarette under a tree. In the meantime, you've got production quotas to meet or a job to finish.

It's not unusual to see laziness amongst young workers new to the job market. They may not be used to buckling down and doing something for hours at a time that doesn't particularly interest them. But we see this amongst older men as well, some of whom spend their entire careers trying to expend as little effort as possible on their jobs.

Lazy men are pretty useless. Pity the woman who marries a guy like this. He won't mow the lawn or look for a job. He won't try to advance himself. He may have trouble hanging onto a job because he's trying to get through life with minimal effort.

There's no honor in this path. If you have lazy tendencies, grab yourself by the back of the neck and start pushing yourself. You'll soon get the habit of making an effort.

Sometimes laziness is caused by physical or mental issues. Things like a bad diet, lack of exercise, too much alcohol, or a low thyroid can make it hard to get off the couch. Perhaps you've had failures in life and have lost the desire to try. All of these things can be remedied and it's up to you to straighten yourself out.

A real man carries his share of the load.

54. Treat your superiors and elders with respect.

"Special respect should be given to Elders, Parents, Teachers, and Community Leaders."

Native American Traditional Code of Ethics

Although men sometimes live as lone wolves, we have also, throughout time, learned to operate in groups, such as the military, the Boy Scouts, and tribal councils. Even a family is a group where a boy can have older siblings, parents, aunts and uncles, and grandparents.

Work

A primary purpose of a group is to secure survival for its members. Family members support each other, co-workers cooperate toward their common goals, and soldiers plan and act to preserve life and property for their fellows, their families, and their nation.

Men are all about survival so it is understood that for these groups to carry out their functions, they must be organized with command channels. Someone has to be in charge and, depending on the size of the organization, there may be a chief and sub-chiefs.

Men also understand that for the group to operate, these chiefs have to be treated with respect and their orders should be followed. Otherwise, all falls apart.

Amongst men of faith, as we see in a number of knights' codes, respect is also paid to God or the Creator, the ultimate "chief."

Throughout history, in virtually all cultures, this same respect has been extended to one's elders—those older than us. The reasoning is simple enough. They have lived longer, experienced more, and carried their share of the load longer. This makes them, presumably, wiser and gives them the right to be treated with respect.

Inevitably, boys and young men challenge this notion. They smart off to their parents or show disrespect to teachers or bosses (commonly behind their backs). Young people frequently challenge the notion that elders or bosses are necessarily wiser.

This isn't new. Nearly 3,000 years ago the Greek poet Hesiod wrote, "I see no hope for the future of our people if they are dependent on the frivolous youth of today, for certainly all youth are reckless beyond words. When I was a boy, we were taught to be discrete and respectful of elders, but the present youth are exceedingly wise [disrespectful] and impatient of restraint."

Of course, there's a grain of truth in this challenge against the wisdom of elders. Older people can have bad judgment or operate with faulty thinking. Or they may be unaware of changing conditions in a society. Occasionally, an elder can behave so dishonorably that respect is scarcely appropriate.

Eventually, however, most disrespectful youth grow up, and through a variety of life lessons, come to understand that one does not have to agree with an elder to show him or her respect. When this youth is twice, three, or four times older, he will see life from a longer track of experience. He will have much to offer—nuggets of wisdom—to those who are younger. And he will learn the real lesson when his wisdom—the hard-won sum of his life experience—is challenged by the youth of his day.

Respect your elders. Most of them have earned it. Also, by doing so, you will have earned the right to ask, in turn, for respect in your older years.

And respect your superiors so that your groups can run smoothly and flourish.

55. Do the hard work, the dirty work, the mechanical work, the dangerous work, and the heavy lifting.

"Never leave a woman to do a man's work."

English proverb

Throughout your life, you will encounter situations that call for a man. A car is in the road and needs a push. A fence has fallen over. An elderly neighbor needs help pulling weightlifting equipment out of her garage. A live raccoon has become stuck in your mother's chimney. Your daughter is trying to pull a stump from the backyard of her new house.

Maybe you don't have time to be the hero, or you'd rather call in a professional or you can't fix cars. That's fine. Just realize that, since you are male, you are the expected solver of these kinds of problems. If you are in an office filled with women and a desk needs moving, they may look to you, and rightfully so.

As we've already established, men's lives are generally more expendable than women or children, so "dangerous" means "give it to a guy."

Because of their structural size and makeup, men are also expected to perform strenuous labor and tolerate physical abuse such as working in the rain, cold, and unhygienic conditions.

As of this writing, less than 3% of American auto or airplane mechanics are women. This is a male domain, not because women can't do it—some better than many men—but because in general, we are hardwired to be builders and fixers of the things we build. Most women would rather not do the more physical, manly labors—for all kinds of reasons. One issue is the social pressure to look attractive. So they don't want to break their nails, scar their skin, ruin their clothes, and mess up their hair. Or maybe they don't care about these things, but they can do the math and realize that someone with a body 50% larger should be the go-to person to pull a stump.

Don't dump these matters on the women and children in your midst. Nature has selected you for the task. When the tire is flat, women's heads will turn your way. This may not always be the case, so do not begrudge a woman who enthusiastically steps in to share the burden. But for the most part, deal with it and be thankful you're so valuable.

56. Always give an honest day's labor.

"Honor lies in honest toil."

Grover Cleveland

One of the classic statements you will hear about a low-class man is, "He never did an honest day's work in his life."

Conversely, one of the most admirable compliments a worker can give one of his fellows—and what every man wants to hear—is, "He always gives 100%."

Work

One of the hallmarks of honorable men is they do their jobs and earn their way. Millions of ordinary guys no one's heard of spend their lives going to work every day and putting in a solid eight (or ten) hours routinely without goofing off, sleeping on the job, or avoiding the responsibilities of their positions. They aren't necessarily geniuses or rock stars. But they show up on time and give their employers a full day's work for a day's pay.

The world counts on these quiet heroes. They keep the trains running and the phones working. They come home tired at the end of the day, knowing they've earned their way.

Now let's look at the man who tries to cheat his way through the day. He spends a half hour in the bathroom reading a magazine. He takes a two-hour lunch. He's a master at looking busy when he's not. He has no pride in his work because he avoids it like the plague.

He might get away with this for a while but eventually his co-workers and his bosses get the picture. There are all kinds of words for a guy like this, none of them flattering.

Men like to be respected. This guy? He doesn't get any because he forces others to carry his load.

Do your job. Earn your pay.

7

DUTY

When I was seven years old, I made the mistake of wandering out of the house on a summer evening to explore the forbidden world of five tough teenagers who hung out at a restaurant a few blocks away. My father wasn't around and I had no older males in my life and I wanted them to like me. They told me to go home and get them some money, so I dutifully looked in my mother's hiding place and took ten dollars from her meager savings.

The boys were thrilled when I brought them the money. They told me to get more and to meet them in an empty lot near the restaurant. But this time my mother saw me approaching her stash and asked what I was doing. I walked away empty-handed and returned to the boys waiting for me in the darkness.

They were not happy when I told them I had nothing. They began pushing me, telling me I had to go back and get more. When I told them I couldn't, one of them pushed me to the ground. When I tried to get up, a foot in my back shoved my face into the dirt.

They began talking excitedly about beating me up. With each statement my heart pounded harder. Finally, one of them suggested they use me sexually. I slowly became aware of the grit on my tongue from the soil in my mouth. All I could see was bits of broken glass gleaming in the moonlight in the dirt around me. I knew I was in deep, deep trouble.

After the sexual comment, one of the boys spoke up. "No, man, leave the kid alone. Let him go." He was obviously the alpha male. The other boys immediately stopped their chatter. "Let him go," I heard again. I took this as a sign to get to my feet. I slowly stepped away in shock and made a shaky retreat home.

I never knew who stood up for me, but obviously it was a young man who, although hanging out with the wrong crowd, still had some sense of honor and duty toward a helpless child in the night.

57. Defend your nation.

"Live to defend Crown and Country and all it holds dear."

Code of Chivalry

Duty

Because of our greater size and natural tendency towards aggressive behavior, males have traditionally carried the duty of defense. In older times, this involved defense of a tribe or village or castle. Today we fight to protect our nation.

The nation is an extended version of the tribe. These are our people. We share a lot in common with them. By protecting the nation, we protect much that we hold dear.

If we don't do that job, we risk losing our families, our property, our rights, and our freedoms.

Some of us may be too old, too young, or otherwise unqualified to serve in the military. We can still support our men and women in uniform. We can still take part in community work, politics, or government to ensure that our constitution is followed and that our country remains true to its governing principles and is protected from destructive influences.

Some men choose not to serve for religious or political reasons. That's a matter of conscience. But it doesn't remove their obligation to defend their nation in some way in its hour of need. Men who let others do the defending while they enjoy a peaceful life on the sidelines are saying they want the benefits of their nation's sanctuary but they are not willing to share in the sacrifice that protection requires.

Our men (and women) in uniform know that they protect the rights of all their countrymen, even those who disrespect or don't support their service to the nation. So these soldiers will not call in your debt.

Only you will know when you see the returning coffins on TV or a veteran in a wheelchair or a Memorial Day ceremony. You will know if you have done your share to defend your nation.

58. If called upon to lead, lead with clarity and set standards of discipline and keep them.

"Ready to Lead, Ready to Follow, Never Quit"

Navy Seal Code

Throughout the history of the human race, most leaders have been men. In current times, women are more and more recognized for their executive skills so we find many of them in leadership positions. But like it or not, most leaders are still men. Presidents, bosses, union leaders, sports managers, supervisors—the odds are that a man holds the position.

Throughout a male's life, he may be asked or required to hold leadership positions of various sorts. He may teach, be a team captain or club president, manage a crew, or just be the head male amongst the guys he hangs out with. Even if he's simply a father, this is a role of power over the life of a child.

Whatever the position of leadership, certain responsibilities will follow. He will impact the futures of the people under him, positively or negatively, in a small or large way. His underlings will look to him to create the group's plans

Duty

or at least ensure they are carried out. He will be expected to be a good example of the organization's persona and ethic. And if things go wrong in his sector of control, he will be expected to exert some muscle to put them right.

There's no escaping these responsibilities once you have assumed or been given a leadership spot. You either deliver or you don't.

If you must lead, do so with clarity. If it's suddenly thrust upon you, it may take some time for you to understand your duties or how you will carry them out, but you need to ensure you grasp these clearly. And you need to be certain that those under you know what you intend to do and what their duties entail.

This can be near impossible if you have to take over for your platoon sergeant in the midst of battle or your father has unexpectedly died, leaving you the family business. But you must do your best or you fail those depending on you.

Maybe you'll get lucky and the orders could simply be, "Do what Joe told you to do," if Joe was a great manager for whom you are taking over in a successful enterprise.

Lastly, ensure those under you know their roles and carry them out. Show by example how to get the job done and, if necessary, show by example what happens to those who don't carry out their duties. In a highly functional group, discipline is often virtually unnecessary. And even when it's required, order can frequently be maintained in a lighthearted fashion. But sometimes a leader has to lay down the law and, though he may be reluctant, he should not hesitate if the situation demands it.

Not every man is a born leader. Many hate the idea. That doesn't change the fact that at any time, one can find himself having to take the reins.

There's much to know about leadership. Entire books have been written on the subject. But as a point of honor, if the crown of leadership is placed on your head, you must lead with clarity and appropriate discipline.

59. Be loyal to your family, group, nation and friends.

"Loyalty to Country, Team and Teammate"

Navy Seal Code

Honor and loyalty are often mentioned in the same sentence because loyalty is the keeping of a promise—a promise of fidelity. Knights were loyal to their king. Men are loyal to their wives and children. A good friend stands by his comrade.

We receive benefits from our arrangements with our girlfriends, wives, employers, nation, and others. For these arrangements to work, however, requires that all parties be faithful. Marriages, companies, governments, and other groups don't function well in the presence of infidelity. Where there should be trust, confidence, and powerful bonds, one finds in-fighting, instability, and suspicion.

Duty

Being honorable means keeping your word as we have already seen. Part of that is your agreement to be loyal to those in your life. This means defending your company against detractors (if you can do so honestly), resisting the urge to flirt when your wife's not around, standing up for your little brother when he's surrounded by bullies, and calling the feds if you see suspected terrorist activity.

Commonly there may not be a spoken agreement. When you tell a girl you want to be in a committed relationship with her, you probably won't say, "I'll be loyal only to you," even if that's what you mean. The same with your company. You likely won't say, "I promise not to tell our competitor our marketing secrets." Whether spoken or not, a respectable man knows when he should be loyal.

Loyalty takes strength. It sometimes means paying your dues when you may not want to or can hardly afford it. But in the long run, there is no other way to live. Loyalty is the gold of human relationships. The faithful man, soldier, and employee is what every woman, nation, and company are looking for. With loyalty, internal peace and harmony can reign. Without it, chaos and bad relations are the rule.

60. Do not desert a friend or ally.

"I will never leave a fallen comrade to fall into the hands of the enemy..."

U.S. Army Rangers Creed

The bond between men can be as powerful as any on earth. After men or boys have worked together side by side, particularly in difficult circumstances, a deep sense of brotherhood and camaraderie often develops. This cultivates an intense loyalty and commitment to protect one another. It is quite ordinary to expect such a "brother" to watch your back, and men have frequently given their lives for their friends.

This sense of protection extends to others in a man's life to whom he is close. These could be neighbors or business associates, male or female. During times of crisis, a man tends to know in his gut who his friends or allies are and if he should lend a hand. But for some people in his life, there is no question—come hell or high water, he needs to be there for them.

The formula for helping your friends is not quite as simple as the military code of "never leave a fallen comrade to fall into the hands of the enemy." That's a straightforward policy with no wiggle room. But in the general run of life, one has to weigh the pros and cons. A friend wants to borrow money but it's more than you can afford. Or in the midst of a riot you have choose between protecting a buddy or your family. Or a fellow employee is in trouble because of violating the law, and you have to choose between bailing him out or letting him learn his lesson.

The bottom line, however, is to stand by your friends as best as you can. Don't desert them. Don't ignore their calls if they are in a crisis. Maybe the fellow is causing his own trouble, and you need to warn him that you can't keep helping him. Fair enough. But for many people in your life, you will get only one request and it will be reasonable or at least doable. On a rare occasion, it may be a tall order but if this friend is worthy enough, you should try to make it happen.

An honorable man stands by his friends.

61. Show compassion and mercy for the weak, the dependent, and the helpless.

"A knight must be merciful without wickedness, affable without treachery, compassionate towards suffering..."

L'Ordene de Chavalerie (13th Century Poem)

A man is a combination of his biological inheritance, the teachings of his culture, and the summary of his own observations. For some males, on a strictly primitive level, compassion and mercy are not necessarily natural. In societies of the past, and in some today, the rule of the day was survival of the fittest. Little concern was shown for those who could not pay their way or who suffered from such things as birth defects, mental derangement, loss of the family's breadwinner or debilitating injury or illness. For the able-bodied to survive, choices were routinely made to leave the weak or elderly to fend for themselves.

The Men's Code of Honor

The same was true with hostile encounters. "Take no prisoners" remains a familiar concept in combat. It means to kill all, show no mercy.

These attitudes remain in the background of most men's consciousness. After all, a tough, demanding environment builds character and strength, even resistance to disease. The concept of "separating the boys from the men" through rigorous screening is one that males routinely live with—and agree with—in sports, the military, business, and a host of other arenas.

But as mankind has advanced, these stark laws of the sword have been tempered by an accumulation of wisdom. In the march of history, alongside history's generals and kings, we eventually find religious leaders and philosophers making their mark. And they are advancing notions that a better life, a fuller life for all is best achieved by showing mercy and compassion for those less fortunate.

Why is it a point of honor for men to do so? Because we have the most power. Men control most of the wealth, strength, property, armies, weapons, and governments in our world. In their sector, they can turn off the faucet of mercy in a heartbeat and make life dark for many. Occasionally, a man like Saddam Hussein or Hitler or a violent husband does so and his brutality becomes a chapter of doom in the lives of those within his grasp.

Because we wield this power, we are left with the sobering reality that we must use it wisely and fairly. Men across political and religious spectrums will differ on what is humane and what is not, but the intention must be there to exercise their might and control judiciously.

Most boys and men know what it's like to torture an insect or small animal, bully a weaker male, intimidate a girl or woman, ridicule someone different from themselves, take from the defenseless, or take advantage of someone dependent on them. We know this because life puts us in positions of power over others and we don't always use it wisely, especially when we are young.

It doesn't take much thought when we look back on those moments to realize there is no honor in such behavior.

You may not be a knight, but there is still plenty of reason for a man to show compassion and mercy for the weak, the dependent, and the helpless.

62. Champion what is right and good.

> "Thou shalt be everywhere and always the champion of the Right and the Good against Injustice and Evil."

The Ten Commandments of the Code of Chivalry

We don't all agree on everything. But when it comes to what is right and good, we find common ground on a great many things.

Justice, honesty, respect for the law, respect for the property of others, protection of children—these and many other things are worth standing up for.

Our lives and those of our family and friends are impacted by negative forces every day. We all work to combat these harmful influences but one way that we mustn't overlook is by promoting the positive.

We can set a good example. Teach our children proper behavior. Compliment and encourage good behavior. Support laws that forward the common good. Defend the innocent. Educate others to do constructive things.

Part of honorable behavior is simply doing the right thing. And that includes being a force for good in the world.

63. Confront and fight evil.

First they came for the communists, and I didn't speak out because I wasn't a communist.

Then they came for the trade unionists, and I didn't speak out because I wasn't a trade unionist.

Then they came for the Jews, and I didn't speak out because I wasn't a Jew.

Then they came for me and there was no one left to speak out for me.

Pastor Martin Niemöller, Nazi Germany

Duty

Of all the mistakes a man will make in his life, one of the greatest will be his failure to confront evil. This can be evil in himself, in another, or in his environment.

Our perception of evil can be masked by our loyalties, our prejudices, our false assumptions, our affections, our ignorance, and even by the ordinary.

As your life rolls out, you find to your dismay that your best friend has been sleeping with his neighbor's wife. Your drinking has been badly affecting your life for five years and you've been in complete denial. Your girlfriend is embezzling money from her company. The candidate you helped get into office is a compulsive liar. Your religious advisor has a habit of forcing himself on women.

These and a thousand other incidents can occur where you may not want to face the fact that you or someone you favor is doing wrong. You will want to explain it away. Or you will excuse it as unimportant.

This happened when Nazis burned massive numbers of bodies in extermination camps. Nearby townspeople watched smoking chimneys and they knew, but somehow they managed to explain it away. While we love to damn these people, the frightening truth is we are all capable of such rationalized thought.

We excuse our friends, our co-workers, our fellow churchgoers, or those who agree with us politically. Or we see suspicious activity and convince ourselves there must be a good reason for it. Or the setting seems so ordinary, like a guy by himself taking pictures of children in a park, that we let it go.

Confronting evil takes a great deal of inner strength. It requires personal certainty about what is right and wrong, the willingness to not go along with the crowd, the courage to look for the truth, and the spine to face the wrath and loss of friendship of those you expose.

Since we are, at our core, protectors, few things are as important in a man's skill set as his ability to confront evil. But few things are as hard.

At some time in your life you will hurt yourself and those close to you because you failed to detect evil in your midst. Even in the next year or two, you might find out that some situation you thought was innocent had crimes or foul play beneath the surface. And you fell for it.

The only lesson to be learned, as we are often told, is that "eternal vigilance is the price of freedom." When it comes to confronting evil, one simply has to learn and relearn to keep one's eyes open. And don't be suckered by the fact that the doer is your close friend or someone you support. Bad behavior is wrong no matter who does it.

Confront evil and deal with it. Don't let it hurt those you care about or rot the foundations of your life.

64. Respect the earth and her life forms.

"Treat the earth and all of her aspects as your mother. Show deep respect for the mineral world, the plant world, and the animal world."

Native American Indian Traditional Code of Ethics

Protecting our environment has been given a bad name in some circles. Some men laughingly call such advocates "tree huggers" or "environmentalist wackos."

Unfortunately, people seeking to create change sometimes use false information or stunts to get the public's attention. It can tarnish their cause as it has with environmentalism.

Truthfully, many sincere men work to protect the natural world. Organizations for hunters, fishermen, campers, and other outdoorsmen commonly encourage members to pick up trash, "leave no trace," respect forestry and game laws, and take measures to avoid polluting their natural playground.

Men pass laws to protect endangered species, set aside areas as wilderness preserves, restrict building, mining and farming in certain areas, and create regulations against air and water pollution—all to safeguard our planet.

As we have repeatedly said, men are guardians of their families and their nations. It is only sensible that they protect the resources and world upon which we all depend. And it is only reasonable that they would want to leave their children and grandchildren the same natural treasures they inherited.

A Native American saying tells us, "Treat the earth well: it was not given to you by your parents, it was loaned to you by your children. We do not inherit the Earth from our Ancestors, we borrow it from our Children."

Studies show that polluted air contributes to health problems in our children. Contaminated water puts chemicals in their (and our) bodies that can cause cancer, hormone imbalances, and other bad effects. Hunting or fishing in excess can wipe out wildlife populations and upset the ecosystem.

Protecting those things we hold dear includes Mother Earth and her inhabitants.

65. Set a good example.

"[I will] use my best endeavors to elevate the standards of the vocation in which I am engaged, and so to conduct my affairs that others in my vocation may find it wise, profitable and conducive to happiness to emulate my example."

Rotary Club Code of Ethics

Duty

One of the greatest responsibilities we carry in life is that, no matter who we are or what our position in life is, we serve as examples to the people around us.

Many men shrug this off with an attitude that they should have the right to behave as they wish, and it's not their problem if someone interprets this as a bad example. Think again, guys.

A father who brags at the dinner table about how he cheated his boss out of a few hundred dollars shouldn't be surprised when his son steals money from Dad's wallet during his sleep.

A man who routinely comes home drunk may get a rude awakening when he gets a call from a hospital that his inebriated teenage daughter has totaled the family car.

Even the bachelor who thinks he can get away with cursing at the neighbor kids can wake up to find profanity drawn on his front door.

Many eyes are upon us. And we represent a great many things to those around us. Kids look to us to learn proper speech, moral conduct, self-defense, money management, and a lot of other lessons. To our neighbors and fellow workers, we represent how our parents raised us, our religion, our political party, our gender, and our nationality, just to name a few things.

We can teach children to behave honorably or dishonorably, simply by how we act. And we can ruin or enhance the reputation of our parents, nation, church, and gender through our behavior.

The honorable man knows this and behaves accordingly.

66. Uphold the tradition of men's honor by expecting other men to be honorable.

"A cadet will not lie, cheat, steal, or tolerate those who do."

West Point Cadet Honor Code

We live in a time where honor is scarcely a topic of discussion at school or work. Instead, we are more familiar with news stories of actors, athletes, and other celebrities who violate the most basic sense of honorable behavior and yet these men often do not, at first, appear to lose status in the public eye.

Still men of honor are quite common. They feed their children, go to work, pay their debts, tell the truth, set wonderful examples, take stock of their behavior regularly, and make many important contributions to our world. They don't get much recognition in the media but they are known by other church members, bosses, fellow soldiers, spouses, children, schoolmates, and employees as the real deal, men who can be counted on to tell it like it is and give you a fair hearing.

Duty

Since honor seems like an old-fashioned notion to so many, it's not common or popular to point out when men are behaving dishonorably. It isn't "cool."

It doesn't matter. Honor is more important than pop culture, and concepts of honor have withstood the test of thousands of years. Part of a man's honor is expecting other men to behave honorably. Never defend or protect dishonor amongst men or boys.

You get a new job and the guys offer to buy you a beer after work. They start joking about how they slap their girlfriends around. Don't let this pass. These guys are jerks and perhaps a single comment from you—something as simple as, "You hit your girlfriend? That's not cool, man..."—could change a man's life.

Peer pressure is very real. If a guy thinks those around him will tolerate his bad behavior, he'll keep it up. You may not be able to change everyone, but when men or boys are called to the carpet by other men for being dishonorable, it hits them where it hurts—right in their manhood. Even if honor isn't popular or something men or boys discuss, they all know the basic rules deep in their souls. They know when they look like weasels, regardless of their excuses.

One of the reasons we see cultural decline, such as so many fatherless families, is because men fail to insist that the men and boys in their vicinity be honorable. When you don't do this, men in general get a bad reputation. And we and those close to us all suffer in ways great and small because so many men have not been pushed to stand tall and assume their responsibilities.

Life isn't perfect. None of us are shining examples 100% of the time. But when it comes to the important stuff, don't keep your mouth shut. If we all hold the line, we can get boys and men to step up their game.

And you can be proud when that boy you set straight years ago comes up to you and says, "Thanks for teaching me how to be a man."

8

THE FALSE CODE

I RETURNED HOME from school one day when I was sixteen to find that my eleven-year-old brother Paul had been taken to the hospital. He had gone to a small store nearby and three adolescents had beaten him to the ground and left him on the sidewalk with his head in a pool of blood. I was enraged. My mother restrained me, telling me not to seek vengeance.

Paul returned home soon with his head bandaged. He told me who his assailants were, names I knew. My father was not around in those days and we had no one to ensure justice was done. My mother, in her eccentric way, felt sorry for the aggressors. I knew it was up to me to seek recourse and to make sure my brother could safely walk the streets again.

A day or so later, I saw two policeman patrolling the neighborhood in a squad car. I waved it down. One of them rolled down the window and asked what the problem was. When I told him, he called me into the back seat. "Listen," said the driver, "these kids are too young for the courts. We can't arrest them at that age. They'll just let 'em go." He looked at me and squinted at the sun shining over my shoulder. "If it was my brother, I'd get myself a baseball bat with a nail in it and take care of this myself. You know what I mean?" His partner nodded in agreement with the recommendation.

My heart sank. I ran that scenario through my head for three seconds and saw that it ended in even more grief for my mother, myself, and lots of others. I thanked the officers and stepped out of the car. I pondered my options. Despite my size—I was six feet tall and 185 pounds when I reached fourteen—I've always been more of a thinker than a fighter, and I tried to come up with a solution that would avoid more bloodshed.

But the officers had made an impression on me. Violence was the only way, it seemed.

Within days, as I walked home from school, I spied one of Paul's attackers in the open. I bolted toward him and he sprang across a vacant lot. I pounced on him and set him down on a fallen telephone pole. At first he denied being involved but he knew I didn't buy it. I was much bigger than him and could have hurt him badly but it wasn't in me. I let him catch his breath. He asked me what I was going to do.

I looked at him in silence for a long time to let the moment take hold. I named the other two boys who had hurt my brother. He squirmed. Slowly and casually I told him that if my brother was ever hurt by anyone again something really bad was going to happen. "How do you think your mom would feel," I asked quietly, "if you didn't come home today, and she got a box in the mail and opened it and found your finger?"

His body went stiff. I saw by his rounded eyes and quivering face that I had made my point. I let him go, not so sure this would be enough to stem the violence.

I wasn't proud of what I did. It was a vicious threat I had no intention of carrying out, a desperate attempt to protect my brother. Had I had the guidance of a sensible adult, I would have known to seek out the parents of the attackers or school authorities and let them straighten out the kids. Unfortunately, I was instructed otherwise and tried to come up with a compromise that didn't involve boys left bleeding on the pavement.

I got extremely lucky and my threat served its purpose. But it could just as easily have caused an escalation in harm against my brother and me. And, like an infection, I had passed onto this cowering boy the idea that violence is best met with threats of more violence. I am left to wonder, at my age now, how many males in his life he passed that false notion to.

The tradition of manly behavior gets handed down through generations of family members, teachers, coaches, and many other mentors and examples that influence a boy's life. Additionally, cultures and families vary a great deal on what they expect of males, and even one's time in history can dictate what people feel a man should do.

Some instructions have been passed down to men, however, that remain in our thinking, yet may not be as honorable as they once were or as constructive as they seem at first glance.

We have included examples of these false rules of conduct here. No doubt other boys and men can come up with more from their lives.

The lesson to be learned from these things is, essentially, to think for ourselves, even if the advice is from trusted sources.

Always avenge your honor.

Part of a man's security and defense is literally the value of his honor—that is, how he is viewed by others. Men of honor are highly valued and can more easily get assistance and have doors opened to them because they can be trusted and are useful to know.

If you slam a man's honor, you devalue him in many ways, so it is natural for a man to get upset about this. And certainly a man should defend his honor by making the truth known or exposing ulterior motives of his detractors.

In older times, it was considered appropriate to take the defamer's head off to avenge your honor. This was also a nice way to burn off some rage.

But we have laws now. And plenty of studies and common sense tell us that stewing in anger and planning the destruction of another is neither healthy nor productive. And there is something called the cycle of violence, where one person hits another, that guy kills him, his son kills that guy, etc., etc.

Avenging your honor is a magnificently romantic concept. But it's not practical in our world. It's not constructive either.

If you are falsely accused or a man rapes your daughter, you have every right to be in a boiling rage. Seek justice, truth, compensation, and whatever else you have a right to. But, unless this is a military situation, don't look for blood. That brings a curse on you that you may not be able to remove.

If he hits you, hit him back.

This is another instruction virtually every boy is given by some male. (Girls are rarely taught this.) It follows the same logic as the rule we just looked at.

When you teach a boy this, you are telling him to handle violence with violence. Also, the cycle of violence comes into play. He hits back, the kid gets his older brother, etc.

Ideally, instead of striking back, a boy should learn to take the matter to the authorities, such as a teacher or nearby adult, who can mete out justice.

Of course, sometimes a boy or man has to physically strike back for his personal safety or to protect others. If that's the case, refer to the rule in the Code that we've covered: "Use force as a last resort, then use it well."

Never rat on your friends no matter what they are doing.

This concept is a perversion of "Do not desert a friend or ally" and "Be loyal to your family, group, nation, and friends."

Sometimes men take advantage of their bonds with their buddies to force them to keep secrets. Bill is cheating on his wife and wants Ed to lie for him. Jason keeps sleeping late and gets Eric to clock in for him at work. Jim has stolen a car and wants to hide it in your garage.

These events sometimes sneak up on you. They happen suddenly and you may not know how to respond so you end up agreeing to something you don't feel right about.

Covering for your friend's lies or crimes is not honorable behavior. It may seem like an act of loyalty if you are really close to this guy and have a lot of history with him, but he's hurting someone unfairly with his actions, and if you help hide his bad deeds, they are your lies and crimes, too.

Part of your contract of loyalty with others is that, for their part, they operate in an upright fashion. If friends, relatives, and co-workers betray that contract with bad behavior, there is a limit as to how far out on a limb you should go for them. You'll know what that is.

"Best friends" doesn't mean you must now serve indefinitely as a sidekick for liars, thieves, and cheaters. Draw the line when your friends behave badly.

Never show your emotions.

Men's genetic and hormonal makeup tends to make them less expressive than females. We may look serious more of the time or not show overt sympathy, joy, or grief when we feel it.

Additionally, men are usually aware of the "masculinity" of their behavior. They generally want to look strong, virile, capable, and in control. This is important behavior for attracting and keeping a mate, looking good to bosses, impressing valuable friends and associates, etc. A man who looks weak can lose respect and these important connections.

In times past and in some cultures today, showing emotions such as grief, kindness, sympathy, or love of beauty could get a man labeled as feminine and lacking in manly qualities. We've all heard it said, "He cried like a woman."

Thus some men have learned to shut down their emotions. Some, also, have been through bad experiences that "taught" them never to cry or express themselves.

The world has changed, however. Expressing one's emotions is not a sign of weakness. Indeed, it can show how strong one's feelings really are. Men can cry over beautiful music, be swept off their feet by a baby's smile, or launch into song at the end of a wonderful date—and they are still men.

Communicating about our feelings enriches our lives immeasurably by allowing us to share our inner world. There is no need to be robbed of that in an effort to be manly.

Never admit you are wrong.

This idea may be thought more than it is spoken. It is the notion that a strong man looks like a fool if he is shown to be wrong, that he can only maintain his masculine appearance by never admitting his mistakes. Most men are not told to do this, but they often learn it by example from other men. It is also part of human nature to not want to admit fault.

This is a great idea for guys who don't like to look stupid, which is all of us, but it's a destructive way to live. Every time you can't admit you're wrong, you carry another secret with you. Your wife can't bring it up. Your friends can't ask you about it. If they do, you get upset or defend it with illogical explanations or lies.

This is, in short, dishonesty. It causes all the trouble that lying does. The truth is, as we have already discussed, it takes courage to admit you are wrong. That act is far more manly and honorable than hiding your mistakes.

The False Code

Never admit to a weakness.

This is a version of the previous false rule of conduct. Again, looking weak can cost a man at work, in romance, and amongst his friends. He wants to appear smart, capable, knowledgeable. Admitting that he has a temper, a drinking problem, or he can't spell can make him look bad. As a result, some men hang onto the idea that to show how strong they are, they need to hide their frailties.

Of course, you may not want to spill your whole private life to your co-workers or the rest of the world, but with certain people in your life, you need to come clean. If you are a terrible money manager but you insist on handling the family's finances because you don't want to look bad, you need to sit down with your wife and swallow your pride.

Admitting to a weakness is the same as admitting you're wrong. It takes courage. The term "Man up" is used to describe, among other things, the act of confessing your faults. Well stated. It is honorable, if painful.

Never let anyone order you around.

This is a gem that has lost men jobs and landed guys in prison because they were showing how tough they were. It's the concept that if you are a real man, you don't take orders from anyone. "Nobody tells me what to do."

Part of this is human nature. Even kids tell us, "You're not the boss of me." We all want to control our own lives, and we don't like being forced to do things we don't like to do.

But men and boys who take this path are confused. They want the benefits of being in our world but they don't want to pay the fare. A civilized society has order in it. There are police, tax collectors, businesses with bosses, and lots of other people who issue rules and orders. If you have any kind of family, it's very likely someone will be regularly telling you what you need to do to fulfill your obligations to your relatives. If you are not willing to take orders, you're going to have to move to Mars, because they are everywhere on Earth.

Refusing orders may impress your fellow gang members as you're being carted off to jail, but when you get there, guess what? You're going to get ordered around.

This is a dead-end path. Smart, honorable men learn to follow sensible orders responsibly and with dignity.

Never show mercy.

This rule has a place in certain military, crime-fighting, or life situations. If an enemy has shown himself to be so physically dangerous that extending mercy could put you at risk, you may need to stick to brute force.

If a criminal or aggressor is shooting at you and will not let you take him peacefully, your non-violent options may be nonexistent. If a business competitor is behaving unfairly to ruin your business, you may need to pull out all the stops, within legal limits, to protect yourself.

In centuries of old, this policy could have been a sound one if you had the experience of showing mercy to your enemies, only to have them come back and hurt you again.

Being merciless brings out an icy ferocity in males (and females), hearkening back to primitive times when we stood on a captive's body and raised his severed head for all to see. It can be a testosterone rush for some men.

However, in most of life's battles, mercy has a place, as does forgiveness, empathy, and understanding. These aren't unmanly qualities, they're smart qualities. They look beyond the battlefield. They look at what will happen next week and next year. They take into account that today's enemies can become tomorrow's allies, and they consider that if we want mercy for ourselves, we have to show it to others.

Abraham Lincoln once remarked, "I have always found that mercy bears richer fruits than strict justice." Enough said.

Strong men are silent men.

Some men don't talk much. They may be shy by nature, not very imaginative, or they may be one of these fellows who prides himself on being the "strong, silent type."

This may look good in movies or on video games but it's not a big winner in real life. A man's unwillingness to communicate does not have much to do with strength. In fact, you really can't accomplish a great deal in life if you're not willing to talk. There's nothing honorable in refusing to engage your girlfriend, wife, or children in conversation.

This can be a tough one for men who are not natural communicators for whatever reason. We can sympathize with their quiet nature and try to understand them. But don't mistake it for macho behavior. There's no connection.

Fear is a sign of cowardice.

Any military commander will tell you that fear is a healthy emotion. Listen to veterans tell their war stories, and almost one for one they'll tell you they were scared to death.

General George Patton probably summed it up best: " All men are afraid in battle. The coward is the one who lets his fear overcome his sense of duty."

Fear can be traumatizing. It can wake you in a cold sweat months or years after it has invaded your soul. But those ghosts are nothing compared to the nightmares that will ride you after acts of cowardice—when your fear ruled your will and you walked (or ran) away from what you knew you had to do.

Never let a woman dominate you.

The subject of male-female control and dominance has become a hot topic in the past century. Women have obtained equal legal rights with men in the Western world and have risen to executive and other powerful positions in government, business, and other organizations. As a result, it's not uncommon for men to have women above them in supervisory roles.

But for all our toughness, we'd still rather be punched in the face than have our male ego bruised. Men, by nature, don't like to be ordered around or made to look weak. For some men, a woman giving them orders hits a nerve and makes them feel emasculated. These same guys don't do well with a pushy wife or girlfriend.

While we can sympathize with their sense of pride, the idea of never letting a woman dominate you is not very practical in today's world. It locks out the ideas of half the population of Earth. It ignores the fact that women can be just as good as men in the executive world. It takes away a wife's or girlfriend's right to exert her will or give her opinion regarding important matters. So while this piece of wisdom— "Never let a woman dominate you…"—may sound good to a bunch of guys around a poker table after the empty beer cans have stacked up, in reality it's bad advice.

A man who is strong in his sense of self can take orders from anyone and really doesn't care who's running the show as long as they're getting the job done.

9

BECOMING A MAN OF HONOR

In the second chapter I related the story of my brush with the law when I was caught stealing with Mike. After leaving the police station that day with my mother, I had a choice to make about changing my bad behavior. I chose poorly.

Not long after that, my mother demanded I no longer spend time with Mike. This was OK with me because I knew he was a corrupt influence. However, Mike didn't like this change and held it against me.

Although I managed to stay away from him, I soon discovered that walking away from Mike was not enough—the inclination to steal was still with me. I had a large, thick coat that my mother had gotten somewhere as used clothing. It was puffy with what looked like sheep's wool on the outside. While I was still hanging with Mike, I discovered a large hole in the coat pocket, allowing my hand to go deep into the lining. One could stuff a large bag of candy into the lining without it being noticeable because the coat was so bulky. I told Mike about my discovery, and we used it several times to steal candy from grocery stores.

After Mike and I had parted ways, I decided to snatch some candy from a small supermarket in the area. I walked in, perused the candy aisle, and grabbed a bag of sweets when no one was looking. I slowly walked past one of the checkout counters with my eye on the door. Just then I had one of the great shocks of my young life.

Mike walked into the store with his new friends. He saw me with my coat on and knew immediately what was happening. An evil smile slowly crossed his lips. He walked toward me and pointed an accusing finger. "Hey, that kid's stealing candy!" he yelled. "It's in his coat!"

All eyes turned to me. Every cell in my body shook, then froze in fear. A strong hand gripped my upper arm from behind. A man glared down at me. "Let me check your pockets, son." I was sunk. He reached in and pulled out the bag of candy.

The man escorted me to the back of the store past a sign that said, "Employees Only." He asked me my name and where I went to school. I answered, assuming he was going to call the police. Instead, he took me to a large bin filled with red potatoes. He stepped over to a nearby table that held a large stack of paper bags with thin cardboard handles. He grabbed a bag and started filling it with potatoes. "Do you see this?" he asked. "This is what I want you to do with these potatoes. Fill each of these bags. While you're doing this, I'm going to decide what I'm going to do with you."

Adrenaline pumped through me and my pulse thumped in my ears. This man acted like something that was a distant memory to me—a father. I was unaccustomed to work. In fact, I hated it and usually weaseled out of it. But not this time.

He walked away and I stood there looking at the potatoes. I picked one up and put it in the bag, then another. I had plenty of time to think as I worked. Over and over I saw the image of Mike's delight at my capture. I thought about my mother and the disappointment she would feel when she found out. I thought of my teacher and what she would say. I looked at the acts I had been committing and realized there had been a time in my life long before when I did not steal. I did not have to be the person I had become. I knew how to be better. If I chose to, I could be, again, the boy who respected other people's property and followed the values he had been taught.

It seemed like two hours before the man returned. I steadied myself for the bad news that the police would be called. His face was not so stern this time. "Are you going to steal from this store again?" he asked.

"No," I said quietly.

"OK. You did a good job. You've made up for the trouble you caused by filling the bags so I'm going to let you go. But

I don't want to see you in here stealing anymore. Do you understand?"

"Yes, sir," I replied. I let out a shuddering sigh as a wave of relief came over me.

"Here," he said. I looked in his hand. It was a candy bar. "Since you worked for it, you earned this. That's how you get things. You don't just take them. Do you understand?"

His face softened. His fatherly concern sank warm and deep into my lonely heart. "Yes, sir," I answered.

He escorted me to the front door, past all the people who'd witnessed my thievery. I walked into the late afternoon chill, grateful for my freedom and determined to change my ways. This time I chose wisely. My stealing days were over.

For most of us, the path to becoming an honorable man starts with a decision. A rare few of us may have had the good fortune to have been raised amongst honorable males and have never known another way of thinking. But for the rest of us, the road is a rough one, filled with mistakes, shameful behavior, bad judgment, self-deception, and failures to keep our commitments to be a better boy or man.

But at some point, some of us "man up." We smoke our last cigarette. We tell the truth about something we've always lied about. For once we apologize after an angry outburst. We keep a promise to ourselves to stop insulting our girlfriend on a daily basis.

The shift can be slow and gradual or it can be quite sudden. But a point comes where we make a successful change in our behavior and then look for other areas of our life where honor has been lacking.

For many men, the exact rules to follow may have been uncertain. Do I lie sometimes or never? Is it OK to cheat certain people but not your close friends? Was my dad right when he told me what people don't know won't hurt them? I got my girlfriend pregnant but whose advice or example do I follow?

It is hoped that in the previous pages, we have been able to clarify the standards that successful, desirable, and honorable men have followed through the ages. It is hoped that these rules of conduct are helpful to men and boys seeking to cut through the fog of uncertainty that is so common in our modern world.

If something in this book doesn't ring true for you, then let your own convictions guide you. You are the master of your destiny and must answer to yourself when all is said and done.

Aristotle once said, "We are what we repeatedly do. Excellence, then, is not an act, but a habit." As you try to behave in an honorable way, you may, at first, meet with failure. Try again. Eventually your better nature will win out and what was once difficult for you will become more natural.

If you repeatedly fail, you may need to do some soul searching. Some false notion in your past or of your own making could be preventing you from lifting yourself to a better place. If you have a habit you can't break of lying to women, perhaps some backward idea is holding this in place, such as, "They'll hate me if I tell them the truth," or "It's OK because I'll never see them again anyway."

The road to honorable behavior gets easier in some ways as you go along. As a man cleans up his act, he often finds that there is an addictive quality to doing the right thing. It feels good and the positive effects are plentiful. And unlike the guilt and hangovers of drugs, alcohol, and other vices, it feels good long afterwards. In short, honorable behavior is its own reward. And the gratification of the honorable life tends to reinforce good behaviors, making it easier to choose the honorable path as time goes on.

It would be great if we could say that once a man has become more honorable he will always be that way. Unfortunately, negative forces in life weaken our resolve routinely and challenge us. Stress, illness, debts, sudden upheavals—these can cause us to resort to old, bad habits or pressure us to take the easy way out.

The best defense against such assaults is to hold in your heart the resolve to live an honorable life. You will never reach perfection. But if you have this resolve, when life's howling winds beat at your door, you will most likely—out of habit and conviction—rely on your code of honor to weather the storm.

Hard though that road may be, the man who walks it will do so with peace of mind, confidence in his step, and a satisfaction that runs deep in his soul, knowing that he has been—in the fullest sense of the word—a real man.

APPENDIX

CODES REFERENCED IN *THE MEN'S CODE OF HONOR*

NUMEROUS CODES OF honor and conduct have been referenced throughout this book. Some of these, such as the Navy Seal Code, are official standards, and others, such as versions of the Code of the West, have become popular through books, web sites, and other media. Some have existed for centuries because they ring true and summarize traditional values of honor.

These codes are listed in the following pages. Where the code is of the traditional variety and not from an organized group, a source is given. Where permission to reprint the code was in question, we have simply listed the name of the code and its source.

Native American Men's Code of Conduct

"I'm sorry" when I make a mistake; and I will show through my actions that I mean it.

I am willing to learn, change and grow.

I will act in a manner that is respectful of myself and others.

I will celebrate my own history and culture, as well as those of others.

I will be accountable for unearned male privilege and strive for gender equality and equity.

I recognize that domestic violence is a community issue, affecting everyone, including men and generations to come.

I will support the development of education across cultures regarding domestic violence as it relates to contemporary societal norms and laws.

I will support community organizations that provide assistance to families, victims and perpetrators.

I will help deliver the message that violence is never an appropriate means of communication or problem solving.

I refuse to abuse.

With a spirit of love and hope, I affirm that I will live by this code, and that I will encourage others to adopt it as well.

(From mensresourcesinternational.org/ uncommonman/ archives/2006/07/native_ american.html)

Appendix

West Point Cadet Honor Code

This code has only one rule:

A cadet will not lie, cheat, steal, or tolerate those who do.

California Institute of Technology Honor Code

This code has only one rule:

No member of the Caltech community shall take unfair advantage of any other member of the Caltech community.

U.S. Army Rangers Creed

Recognizing that I volunteered as a Ranger, fully knowing the hazards of my chosen profession, I will always endeavor to uphold the prestige, honor, and high esprit de corps of the Rangers.

 Acknowledging the fact that a Ranger is a more elite soldier who arrives at the cutting edge of battle by land, sea, or air, I accept the fact that as a Ranger my country expects me to move further, faster, and fight harder than any other soldier.

Never shall I fail my comrades. I will always keep myself mentally alert, physically strong, and morally straight and I will shoulder more than my share of the task whatever it may be, one hundred percent and then some.

Gallantly will I show the world that I am a specially selected and well trained soldier. My courtesy to superior officers, neatness of dress, and care of equipment shall set the example for others to follow.

Energetically will I meet the enemies of my country. I shall defeat them on the field of battle for I am better trained and will fight with all my might. Surrender is not a Ranger word. I will never leave a fallen comrade to fall into the hands of the enemy and under no circumstances will I ever embarrass my country.

Readily will I display the intestinal fortitude required to fight on to the Ranger objective and complete the mission, though I be the lone survivor.

Boy Scouts of America's Scout Law

A Scout is Trustworthy.

A Scout tells the truth. He is honest, and he keeps his promises. People can depend on him.

A Scout is Loyal.

A Scout is true to his family, friends, Scout leaders, school, and nation.

Appendix

A Scout is Helpful.

A Scout cares about other people. He willingly volunteers to help others without expecting payment or reward.

A Scout is Friendly.

A Scout is a friend to all. He is a brother to other Scouts. He offers his friendship to people of all races and nations, and respects them even if their beliefs and customs are different from his own.

A Scout is Courteous.

A Scout is polite to everyone regardless of age or position. He knows that using good manners makes it easier for people to get along.

A Scout is Kind.

A Scout knows there is strength in being gentle. He treats others as he wants to be treated. Without good reason, he does not harm or kill any living thing.

A Scout is Obedient.

A Scout follows the rules of his family, school, and troop. He obeys the laws of his community and country. If he thinks these rules and laws are unfair, he tries to have them changed in an orderly manner rather than disobeying them.

The Men's Code of Honor

A Scout is Cheerful.

A Scout looks for the bright side of life. He cheerfully does tasks that come his way. He tries to make others happy.

A Scout is Thrifty.

A Scout works to pay his own way and to help others. He saves for the future. He protects and conserves natural resources. He carefully uses time and property.

A Scout is Brave.

A Scout can face danger although he is afraid. He has the courage to stand for what he thinks is right even if others laugh at him or threaten him.

A Scout is Clean.

A Scout keeps his body and mind fit and clean. He chooses the company of those who live by high standards. He helps keep his home and community clean.

A Scout is Reverent.

A Scout is reverent toward God. He is faithful in his religious duties. He respects the beliefs of others.

(The Boy Scouts of America's "Scout Law" is excerpted from the *Boy Scout Handbook*, 11th ed.

Appendix

Copyright © 1998 Boy Scouts of America. Used with permission.)

Military Code of Conduct

Article I: I am an American, fighting in the armed forces which guard my country and our way of life. I am prepared to give my life in their defense.

Article II: I will never surrender of my own free will. If in command I will never surrender the members of my command while they still have the means to resist.

Article III: If I am captured, I will continue to resist by all means available. I will make every effort to escape and aid others to escape. I will accept neither parole nor special favors from the enemy.

Article IV: If I become a prisoner of war, I will keep faith with my fellow prisoners. I will give no information nor take part in any action which might be harmful to my comrades. If I am senior, I will take command. If not, I will obey the lawful orders of those appointed over me and will back them up in every way.

Article V: When questioned, should I become a prisoner of war, I am required to give name, rank, service, number, and date of birth. I will evade answering further questions to the utmost of my ability. I will make no oral or written statements disloyal to my country and its allies or harmful to their cause.

Article VI: I will never forget that I am an American, responsible for my actions, and dedicated to the principles which made my country free. I will trust in my God and in the United States of America.

The Sailor's Creed

I am a United States Sailor.

I will support and defend the Constitution of the United States of America and I will obey the orders of those appointed over me.

I represent the fighting spirit of the Navy and those who have gone before me to defend freedom and democracy around the world.

I proudly serve my country's Navy combat team with honor, courage, and commitment.

I am committed to excellence and the fair treatment of all.

Appendix

Core Values of the United States Navy

Honor: "I will bear true faith and allegiance ..." Accordingly, we will: Conduct ourselves in the highest ethical manner in all relationships with peers, superiors and subordinates; Be honest and truthful in our dealings with each other, and with those outside the Navy; Be willing to make honest recommendations and accept those of junior personnel; Encourage new ideas and deliver the bad news, even when it is unpopular; Abide by an uncompromising code of integrity, taking responsibility for our actions and keeping our word; Fulfill or exceed our legal and ethical responsibilities in our public and personal lives twenty-four hours a day. Illegal or improper behavior or even the appearance of such behavior will not be tolerated. We are accountable for our professional and personal behavior. We will be mindful of the privilege to serve our fellow Americans.

Courage: "I will support and defend ..." Accordingly, we will have: courage to meet the demands of our profession and the mission when it is hazardous, demanding, or otherwise difficult; Make decisions in the best interest of the navy and the nation, without regard to personal consequences; Meet these challenges while adhering to a higher standard of personal conduct and decency; Be loyal to our nation, ensuring the resources entrusted to us are used in an honest, careful, and efficient way. Courage is the value that gives us the moral and mental strength to do what is right, even in the face of personal or professional adversity.

Commitment: "I will obey the orders ..." Accordingly, we will: Demand respect up and down the chain of command; Care for the safety, professional, personal and spiritual well-being of our people; Show respect toward all people without regard to race, religion, or gender; Treat each individual with human dignity; Be committed to positive change and constant improvement; Exhibit the highest degree of moral character, technical excellence, quality and competence in what we have been trained to do. The day-to-day duty of every Navy man and woman is to work together as a team to improve the quality of our work, our people and ourselves.

Code of the West (James P. Owen)

1. Live each day with courage.
2. Take pride in your work.
3. Always finish what you start.
4. Do what has to be done.

Appendix

5. Be tough, but fair.

6. When you make a promise, keep it.

7. Ride for the brand.

8. Talk less and say more.

9. Remember that some things aren't for sale.

10. Know where to draw the line.

(Reprinted with permission from the book *Cowboy Ethics: What Wall Street Can Learn from the Code of the West* by James P. Owen, copyright © 2005. From http://www.elvaquero.com/The_Cowboy_Code.htm)

U.S. Navy Seal Code

Loyalty to Country, Team and Teammate

Serve with Honor and Integrity On and Off the Battlefield

Ready to Lead, Ready to Follow, Never Quit

Take responsibility for your actions and the actions of your teammates

Excel as Warriors through Discipline and Innovation

Train for War, Fight to Win, Defeat our Nation's Enemies

Earn your Trident everyday

Code of the West (Texas Bix Bender)

(From the book *Don't Squat With Your Spurs On: A Cowboy's Guide to Life* by Texas Bix Bender. From http://www.reloadammo.com/westcode.htm)

The Ten Commandments of the Code of Chivalry

Thou shalt believe all that the Church teaches, and shalt observe all its directions.

Thou shalt defend the Church.

Thou shalt respect all weaknesses, and shalt constitute thyself the defender of them.

Thou shalt love the country in which thou wast born.

Thou shalt not recoil before thine enemy.

Thou shalt make war against the Infidel without cessation, and without mercy.

Thou shalt perform scrupulously thy feudal duties, if they be not contrary to the laws of God.

Thou shalt never lie, and shall remain faithful to thy pledged word.

Appendix

Thou shalt be generous, and give largess to everyone.

Thou shalt be everywhere and always the champion of the Right and the Good against Injustice and Evil.

(From the book *Chivalry* by Leon Gautier. From http://www.medieval-spell.com/Medieval-Code-of-Chivalry.html)

The Polish Knights' Movement Regulations (Regula Rycerska)

(Translated from Polish: From http://www.rycerzesztum.pl/regularycerska.html)

Oath of Knighthood

(From www.medieval-life-and-times.info/medieval-knights/knighthood-ceremony.htm)

The Code of Chivalry

This is the only code in *The Men's Code of Honor* drawn from a work of fiction: a game called the *Rifts: England Supplement*, published by Palladium Books (www.palladiumbooks.com). However, the Code of Chivalry is clearly based on traditional codes of knighthood. It is widely cited on the internet, indicating that it is an inspiration to many. One site where it may be found is http://www.kisd.org/khs/English/Web%20Quests/king_arthur.htm.

From L'Ordene de Chavalerie

"There were tall and strong,

The Handsome and robust,

The loyal, the valiant and bold…..

A knight must be merciful without wickedness,

Affable without treachery,

Compassionate towards suffering,

….. and openhanded.

He must be ready to help the needy

And confound robbers and murderers,

A just judge without favour or hate.

He must prefer death to dishonor.

He must protect the Holy Church for she cannot defend herself."

(13th Century Poem—Author Unknown)

Appendix

The Extension Workers' Code of 1922

This code is, unfortunately, far too lengthy to include in this appendix. However, it is a remarkable list of commonsense practices for guiding one's conduct in life and is well worth reading. It reminds us of how little has changed about human conduct in the near-century since it was written.

(Note: Extension workers assist farm people, through educational procedures, in improving farming methods and techniques.)

(From: www.ksre.ksu.edu/historicpublications/pubs/exbul33.pdf)

Native American Indian Traditional Code of Ethics

1. Each morning upon rising, and each evening before sleeping, give thanks for the life within you and for all life, for the good things the Creator has given you and for the opportunity to grow a little more each day. Consider your thoughts and actions of the past day and seek for the courage and strength to be a better person. Seek for the things that will benefit others (everyone).

Respect: Respect means "To feel or show honor or esteem for someone or something; to consider the well being of, or to treat someone or something with deference or courtesy." Showing respect is a basic law of life.

a. Treat every person from the tiniest child to the oldest elder with respect at all times.

b. Special respect should be given to Elders, Parents, Teachers, and Community Leaders.

c. No person should be made to feel "put down" by you; avoid hurting other hearts, as you would avoid a deadly poison.

d. Touch nothing that belongs to someone else (especially Sacred Objects) without permission, or an understanding between you.

e. Respect the privacy of every person; never intrude on a person's quiet moment or personal space.

f. Never walk between people that are conversing.

g. Never interrupt people who are conversing.

h. Speak in a soft voice, especially when you are in the presence of Elders, strangers or others to whom special respect is due.

i. Do not speak unless invited to do so at gatherings where Elders are present (except to ask what is expected of you, should you be in doubt).

j. Never speak about others in a negative way, whether they are present or not.

k. Treat the earth and all of her aspects as your mother. Show deep respect for the mineral world, the plant world, and the animal world.

Do nothing to pollute our Mother, rise up with wisdom to defend her.

l. Show deep respect for the beliefs and religion of others.

m. Listen with courtesy to what others say, even if you feel that what they are saying is worthless. Listen with your heart.

n. Respect the wisdom of the people in council. Once you give an idea to a council meeting it no longer belongs to you. It belongs to the people. Respect demands that you listen intently to the ideas of others in council and that you do not insist that your idea prevail. Indeed you should freely support the ideas of others if they are true and good, even if those ideas are quite different from the ones you have contributed. The clash of ideas brings forth the Spark of Truth.

3. Once a council has decided something in unity, respect demands that no one speak secretly against what has been

decided. If the council has made an error, that error will become apparent to everyone in its own time.

4. Be truthful at all times, and under all conditions.

5. Always treat your guests with honor and consideration. Give of your best food, your best blankets, the best part of your house, and your best service to your guests.

6. The hurt of one is the hurt of all; the honor of one is the honor of all.

7. Receive strangers and outsiders with a loving heart and as members of the human family.

8. All the races and tribes in the world are like the different colored flowers of one meadow. All are beautiful. As children of the Creator they must all be respected.

9. To serve others, to be of some use to family, community, nation, and the world are one of the main purposes for which human beings have been created. Do not fill yourself with your own affairs and forget your most important talks. True happiness comes only to those who dedicate their lives to the service of others.

10. Observe moderation and balance in all things.

11. Know those things that lead to your well being, and those things that lead to your destruction.

Appendix

12. Listen to and follow the guidance given to your heart. Expect guidance to come in many forms; in prayer, in dreams, in times of quiet solitude, and in the words and deeds of wise Elders and friends.

(From www.shamanswell.org/shaman/native-american-indian-traditional-code-ethics. Originally published in the book *The Sacred Tree* by the Four Worlds Development Project, www.fwii.net.)

Native American Code of Ethics

1. Rise with the sun to pray. Pray alone. Pray often. The Great Spirit will listen, if you only speak.

2. Be tolerant of those who are lost on their path. Ignorance, conceit, anger, jealousy and greed stem from a lost soul. Pray that they will find guidance.

3. Search for yourself, by yourself. Do not allow others to make your path for you. It is your road, and yours alone. Others may walk it with you, but no one can walk it for you.

4. Treat the guests in your home with much consideration. Serve them the best food, give them the best bed and treat them with respect and honor.

5. Do not take what is not yours whether from a person, a community, the wilderness or from a culture. It was not earned nor given. It is not yours.

6. Respect all things that are placed upon this earth whether it be people or plant.

7. Honor other people's thoughts, wishes and words. Never interrupt another or mock or rudely mimic them. Allow each person the right to personal expression.

8. Never speak of others in a bad way. The negative energy that you put out into the universe will multiply when it returns to you.

9. All persons make mistakes. And all mistakes can be forgiven.

10. Bad thoughts cause illness of the mind, body and spirit. Practice optimism.

11. Nature is not FOR us, it is a PART of us. They are part of your worldly family.

12. Children are the seeds of our future. Plant love in their hearts and water them with wisdom and life's lessons. When they are grown, give them space to grow.

13. Avoid hurting the hearts of others. The poison of your pain will return to you.

14. Be truthful at all times. Honesty is the test of ones will within this universe.

15. Keep yourself balanced. Your Mental self, Spiritual self, Emotional self, and Physical self—all need to be strong, pure

and healthy. Work out the body to strengthen the mind. Grow rich in spirit to cure emotional ails.

16. Make conscious decisions as to who you will be and how you will react. Be responsible for your own actions.

17. Respect the privacy and personal space of others. Do not touch the personal property of others—especially sacred and religious objects. This is forbidden.

18. Be true to yourself first. You cannot nurture and help others if you cannot nurture and help yourself first.

19. Respect others religious beliefs. Do not force your belief on others.

20. Share your good fortune with others. Participate in charity.

(Published in the Inter-Tribal Times, 1994. From www.nativevillage.org/Inspiration/native_american_code_of_ethics__.htm. Taken from the book *The Sacred Tree* from Four Worlds International Institute [www.fwii.net].)

The Articles of John Philips
(Captain of the pirate ship *Revenge*)

1. Every man shall obey civil Command; the Captain shall have one full share and a half in all Prizes; the Master,

Carpenter, Boatswain and Gunner shall have one Share and quarter.

2. If any man shall offer to run away, or keep any Secret from the Company, he shall be marroon'd with one Bottle of Powder, one Bottle of Water, one small Arm and shot.

3. If any Man shall steel any Thing in the Company, or game, to the Value of a Piece of Eight, he shall be marroon'd or shot. If at any Time we should meet another Marrooner (that is Pyrate) that Man that shall sign his Articles without the Consent of our Company, shall suffer such Punishment as the Captain and Company shall think fit.

4. That Man that shall strike another whilst these Articles are in force, shall receive Mose's Law (that is 40 stripes lacking one) on the bare Back.

5. That Man that shall snap his Arms, or smoak Tobacco in the Hold, without a cap to his Pipe, or carry a Candle lighted without a Lanthorn, shall suffer the same Punishment as in the former Article.

6. That Man that shall not keep his Arms clean, fit for an Engagement, or neglect his Business, shall be cut off from his Share, and suffer such other Punishment as the Captain and the Company shall think fit.

7. If any Man shall lose a Joint in time of an Engagement he shall have 400 pieces of Eight; if a limb 800.

Appendix

8. If at any time you meet with a prudent Woman, that Man that offers to meddle with her, without her Consent, shall suffer present Death.

(British) Armed Forces Code of Social Conduct

1. This Code of Social Conduct explains the Armed Forces' policy on personal relationships involving Service personnel. It applies to all members of the Armed Forces regardless of their gender (including gender reassignment status), sexual orientation, race, religion, belief, ability, rank or status. The provisions apply equally to members of the Regular and the Reserve Forces. The Code of Social Conduct should be read in conjunction with the Ministry of Defence's Unified Diversity Strategy.

2. In the area of personal relationships, the overriding operational imperative to sustain team cohesion and to maintain trust and loyalty between commanders and those they command imposes a need for standards of social behaviour that are more demanding than those required by society at large. Such demands are equally necessary during peacetime and on operations. Examples of behaviour that can undermine such trust and cohesion, and therefore damage the morale or discipline of a unit (and hence its operational effectiveness) include:

- unwelcome sexual attention in the form of physical or verbal conduct
- over-familiarity with the spouses, civil partners or partners of other Service personnel
- displays of affection which might cause offence to others
- behaviour which damages or puts at risk the marriage, civil partnership or personal relationships of Service personnel or civilian colleagues within the wider defence community
- misuse of rank and taking advantage of subordinates
- probing into a person's private life and relationships

It is important to acknowledge in the tightly knit military community a need for mutual respect and a requirement to avoid conduct which offends or causes distress to others. Each case will be judged on an individual basis.

3. It is not practicable to list every type of conduct that may constitute social misbehaviour. The seriousness with which misconduct will be regarded will depend on the individual circumstances and the potential for adversely affecting operational effectiveness and team cohesion. Nevertheless, misconduct involving abuse of position, trust or rank, or

Appendix

taking advantage of an individual's separation, will be viewed as being particularly serious.

4. Unacceptable social conduct requires prompt and positive action to prevent damage. Timely advice and informal action can often prevent a situation developing to the point where it could:

- impact adversely on third parties; and/or
- impair the effectiveness of a Service individual or unit
- result in damage to corporate image or reputation

However, on occasion it may be appropriate to proceed directly to formal administrative or disciplinary action. Such action is always to be proportionate to the seriousness of the misconduct. It may constitute a formal warning, official censure, the re-assignment of one or more of the parties involved or disciplinary action. In particularly serious cases, or where an individual persists with, or has a history of acts of social misconduct, formal disciplinary or administrative action may be taken, which might lead to termination of service.

The Service Test

5. When considering possible cases of social misconduct, and in determining whether the Service has a duty to intervene in the personal lives of its personnel, Commanding

Officers at every level must consider each case against the following Service Test:

"Have the actions or behaviour of an individual adversely impacted or are they likely to impact on the efficiency or operational effectiveness of the Service?"

This Service Test lies at the heart of the Armed Forces' Code of Social Conduct; it is equally applicable to all forms of conduct, including behaviour while not on duty. In assessing whether to take action, Commanding Officers will consider a series of key criteria. This will establish the seriousness of the misconduct and its impact on operational effectiveness and thus the appropriate and proportionate level of sanction. Each of the Services has its own statement on values and standards.

Diversity Impact Assessment

This policy does not discriminate on grounds of race, ethnic origin, religion, belief, sexual orientation or social background. Neither does it discriminate on grounds of gender, disability or age, insofar as the legislation applies to the Armed Forces. The Diversity Impact Assessment is held by the "Code of Social Conduct" Policy sponsor.

Appendix

The Rotary Code of Ethics
For Businessmen of All Lines

(From http://www.rotaryfirst100.org/history/headings/ethics.htm)

Thirteenth Century Code of Chivalry

By the thirteen century, a "Code of chivalry" or "Knightly behavior" emerged:

- largesse or generosity.
- pity or compassion.
- franchise or a free and frank spirit.
- courtoise or courtliness, especially to women.
- Thou shalt avoid avarice like the plague and shall embrace its opposite.
- Thou shalt speak no evil.
- Thou shalt be all things polite and courteous.
- Courage in face of hardships.
- Military Prowess in the defense of their country.
- Have virtue even though tempted to brag about the love of your own achievements.
- Respect for the truth and what is right.

- The ability to admit fault, when proved wrong.
- Benevolence towards all thy brethren, including to defend the weak from oppression.
- Good disposition towards all.
- Be careful to avoid any kind of falsehood.
- Service to God and the teachings of their own religion.
- A lack of jealousy for the achievements of others.
- Loyalty to their King or Master.

(From www.angelfire.com/realm/StStanislas/Chivalry.html and www.courtlylives.com by Margaret Odrowaz-Sypniewska)

Gentleman's Code of Conduct

1. Make attention to detail a way of life.
2. Take pride in your appearance.
3. Keep leather shoes highly polished.
4. Spend enough time on personal grooming.
5. Understand that sacrificing quantity for quality is no sacrifice.
6. Never follow fads, just update classic fashions.
7. Keep jewelry to a minimum (Watch, wedding ring (if relevant!) & maybe a subtle neck chain if tasteful).

Appendix

8. Have the right handshake (no bone crunching or limp wristed efforts).
9. Enjoy your drink, but don't get drunk.
10. Be up to date on current affairs so you always have something relevant to talk about.
11. If you invite someone on a date, you pick up the bill.
12. Don't swear or use offensive language in the wrong company.
13. Always keep your environment clean & tidy (desk, car, home).
14. Develop and use your network.
15. Get to know your tailor.
16. Get to know your barber.
17. Always show genuine respect of others.
18. Know when to stand for a lady.
19. Understand your values and stick to them.
20. Know your national anthem.
21. Understand why less is more.
22. Learn how to identify quality (products, services, advice).
23. Never miss an opportunity to gain new life experiences.

(By Steve Mitchell from www.themitchelli.com/2010/08/gentlemans-code)

Jesuit Athlete's Code of Conduct

Being a Jesuit Athlete is a student choice and thereby a privilege, one that along with being a great honor, carries with it responsibilities. The following are expected of a Jesuit Athlete:

1. Jesuit athletes will be intense competitors on the field or court, but are expected to conduct themselves as gentlemen at all times and strive to model their behavior after Jesuit ideals.

2. Jesuit athletes are to display positive leadership at all times in our school and around the community.

3. Jesuit athletes are to strive for the highest in moral and spiritual values.

4. When travelling to compete against other schools, Jesuit athletes will represent themselves and their teams in a manner that reflects the Jesuit values and ideals.

5. Jesuit athletes recognize that they must demonstrate Intellectual Competence, and fulfill all other areas of the Jesuit Profile, as a pre-requisite to athletic competition.

Appendix

As a Jesuit athlete, our young men have an image to reflect: one of positive leadership, character, responsibility, competitive spirit, and integrity.

Students are not required to take part in any contest or activity. Therefore, it is imperative that all students taking part in athletics understand the following responsibilities and rules and that the coaches of that athletic program and the athletic director have the right to remove that privilege.

Training

The following rules apply to all athletes at all times:

1. No use of tobacco of any kind.

2. No drinking of alcoholic beverages of any kind.

3. No use of illegal drugs (marijuana, narcotics, steroids, etc.).

These rules apply to all athletes during each of their athletic seasons. Being an athlete at Jesuit is a commitment that goes beyond the formal season. This includes all year round conditioning programs mandated by the coaching staffs. Violations may result in the school imposing serious consequences.

Other Rules

The athlete must obey all team rules given to him by his coach in a particular sport.

(This is the first half of the code. It may be found in full at http://www.jesuitcp.org/document.doc?id=979. Our thanks to the source, the Jesuit College Preparatory School of Dallas, for permission to reprint.)

Benjamin Franklin's Thirteen Virtues of Life

Temperance: Eat not to dullness; drink not to elevation.

Silence: Speak not but what may benefit others or yourself; avoid trifling conversation.

Order: Let all your things have their places; let each part of your business have its time.

Resolution: Resolve to perform what you ought; perform without fail what you resolve.

Frugality: Make no expense but to do good to others or yourself; i.e., waste nothing.

Industry: Lose no time; be always employed in something useful; cut off all unnecessary actions.

Sincerity: Use no hurtful deceit; think innocently and justly, and, if you speak, speak accordingly.

Justice: Wrong none by doing injuries, or omitting the benefits that are your duty.

Moderation: Avoid extremes; forbear resenting injuries so much as you think they deserve.

Appendix

Cleanliness: Tolerate no uncleanliness in body, cloths, or habitation.

Tranquility: Be not disturbed at trifles, or at accidents common or unavoidable.

Chastity: Rarely use venery but for health or offspring, never to dullness, weakness, or the injury of your own or another's peace or reputation.

Humility: Imitate Jesus and Socrates.

Knight's Code of Chivalry

- To fear God and maintain His Church
- To serve the liege lord in valour and faith
- To protect the weak and defenceless
- To give succour to widows and orphans
- To refrain from the wanton giving of offence
- To live by honour and for glory
- To despise pecuniary reward
- To fight for the welfare of all
- To obey those placed in authority
- To guard the honour of fellow knights
- To eschew unfairness, meanness and deceit
- To keep faith

- At all times to speak the truth
- To persevere to the end in any enterprise begun
- To respect the honour of women
- Never to refuse a challenge from an equal
- Never to turn the back upon a foe

(From www.middle-ages.org.uk/knights-code-of-chivalry.htm)

The Pirate Code of Conduct

(From http://library.thinkquest.org/05aug/01841/code.html)

Appendix

ADDITIONAL RESOURCES

The Knight's Code:

www.mistychouse.com/Knight's-code/knight's-code-only.htm

Association for Renaissance Martial Arts Youth Code of Chivalry:

www.thearma.org/Youth/Youth.htm

The Oath of Enlistment
Gene Autry's Cowboy Code
Lone Ranger Creed
Roy Roger's Riders Club Rules
National Rifle Association Hunter's Code of Ethics
Butler's Guild Code of Honor
The Articles of Edward Low
The Articles of Bartholomew Roberts

QUICK ORDER FORM

Fax orders: 626-791-7867. Send this form.

Telephone orders: Call 626-204-0279

Email orders: orders@whispercanyon.net

Postal orders: Whisper Canyon Publishing, 787 W. Woodbury Rd., #2, Altadena, CA 91001, USA

Please send _____ copies of *The Men's Code of Honor* @ $14.95 each.

Name _____

Address _____

City_____State_____Zip _____

Telephone _____

Email address _____

Sales tax: Please add 8.75% for products shipped to California addresses.

Shipping by air to U.S.: $4 for first book and $2 for each additional book.

International: $9.00 for first book and $5 for each additional book.

Credit Card No. _____

Address (if different from above): _____

_____Exp. Date: _____